2nd Edition

Asking the Right Questions

2nd Edition

Asking the Right Questions

Techniques for Collaboration and School Change

Edie L. Holcomb

CORWIN PRESS, INC.
A Sage Publications Company
Thousand Oaks, California

For information address:

Corwin Press, Inc.
A Sage Publications Company
2455 Teller Road
Thousand Oaks, California 91320
E-mail: order@corwin.sagepub.com

Sage Publications Ltd.
6 Bonhill Street
London EC2A 4PU
United Kingdom

Sage Publications India Pvt. Ltd.
M-32 Market
Greater Kailash I
New Delhi 110 048 India

Printed in the United States of America

Library of Congress Cataloging-in-Publication Data

Holcomb, Edie L.
    Asking the right questions: Techniques for collaboration and school change / Edie L. Holcomb. — 2nd ed.
        p.   cm.
    Includes bibliographical references and index.
    ISBN 0-7619-7675-2 (cloth: alk. paper)
    ISBN 0-7619-7676-0 (pbk.: alk. paper)
    1. Group work in education—United States.   2. Team learning approach in education—United States.   3. Educational change—United States.
    4. School management and organization—United States.   I. Title.
    LB1032 .H64   2000
    371.39'5—dc21   00-010235

This book is printed on acid-free paper.

05   06   07   7   6   5   4

Corwin Editorial Assistant:	Kylee Liegl
Production Editor:	Nevair Kabakian
Editorial Assistant:	Candice Crosetti
Typesetter/Designer:	Lynn Miyata
Indexer:	Molly Hall
Cover Designer:	Michelle Lee

Contents

Foreword

If you don't have a hammer,
a shoe will do.

That myth is dispelled in this book that offers assistance to school-based teams and their leaders as they guide and support schools in their change and improvement efforts. Most everyone agrees that schools should be about the business of increasing their effectiveness, and many volumes have been written to advance this goal. None, however, has provided the leaders and facilitators of the school improvement process with the kind of down-to-earth information and guidance for conducting the day-to-day work of school change and improvement that this book does.

Asking the Right Questions: Techniques for Collaboration and School Change is both elegantly written and eminently easy to read. Its practical content entices the school leader along, to learn what this volume has to offer: both wit and wisdom about a finely honed compendium of tools and techniques, along with tips and strategies for when and how to use them.

In this second edition, Edie Holcomb richly expands her offerings to school change leaders. The additional examples, illustrations, and stories provide the user of the material with a stockpile of new information and applications; the benefit to school leaders and their teams is an enhanced repertoire of "how to do it's" and when and why "to do it." The value added of the new edition is access to 50% more of Holcomb's advice and counsel for successfully conducting school change and improvement.

The book is organized thoughtfully around five questions that represent phases or stages of the school improvement process:

- ◆ Where are we now?

- ◆ Where do we want to go?

- ◆ How will we get there?

◆ How will we know we are (getting) there?

◆ How will we sustain the focus and momentum?

Tools that are most relevant to each of the phases are identified. A consistent outline identifies each tool's purpose, when to use it, who to involve, and materials that are needed. It also provides tips for facilitators and an example of each tool's application. This arrangement and description of the tools make for user-friendly accessibility of the information by school improvement leaders and facilitators. A sample of the tools includes histograms, surveys, run charts, weighted voting, force field analysis, decision matrices, and many others. Some of these tools will be familiar to school leadership teams, but their applications may be new. Others will be unfamiliar but available for new learning.

No one is better able to provide school leaders with tools that add rigor and precision to their daily operations than Edie Holcomb. She has been a campus leader of school reform and has experienced and studied the process at the personal and practical learning levels. She has trained and developed others, preparing them for the role of leaders of change. To do this, she has developed training materials and activities and has served as a national and an international presenter and disseminator of the materials.

In the text, her stories of practice at the campus and district levels come from personal experiences that encompass a wide range of roles and responsibilities. Her use of colorful metaphors contributes richly to the descriptions and explanations of the requirements of the school change journey—a trip she has made many times. Her own hands-on experiences are reflected in the information she shares, for example, in her reference to the "TYNT-NYNT syndrome: 'this year's new thing' soon replaced by 'next year's new thing'" (p. 8).

In short, Edie Holcomb has been in the trenches as a school practitioner learning about change. But she also has taken the opportunity as a school change trainer to analyze and study the process from the developer's perspective. In addition, she has been a student of the research literature, enhancing her knowledge base while serving on faculty in higher education. These various plateaus and perspectives of the world have contributed to her thoughtful observations and advice such as, "Only through sensitivity to the past can change agents link innovation with events remembered fondly and disassociate new practices from those that have left bitter legacies" (p. 18). She tells it like an insider—and an outsider—as one who has been in both places.

With this broad background, Holcomb makes a rich contribution to the resources for school change leaders and facilitators. All persons who hold responsibility for guiding and supporting schools in their reform and improvement endeavors will find much of value in this book.

—Shirley M. Hord
Southwest Educational Development Laboratory
Austin, Texas

Acknowledgments

The first edition of this book was dedicated to the memory of my minister-father, Warren E. Holcomb, who continued to nurture me through adulthood, providing daily demonstrations of lifelong learning and servant leadership. This edition honors my mother, Edith, who has continued her solo journey with courage and dignity, a faithful first-grade volunteer at 82.

It could not have been written without the opportunities, assistance, and support provided by many individuals and groups. I offer my apologies to those I will inevitably omit and extend grateful thanks to the following:

Lee F. Olsen, my husband, research assistant, cheerleader, and coach

Dave Pedersen and Jody Bublitz, technical assistants, for turning my scribbles into a matrix and my wall charts into figures

Richard Rossmiller, professor emeritus, University of Wisconsin—former boss, continuing colleague, role model, and friend

Barb Furlong, who first suggested I develop a chart and then told me to write about it

Dennis Glaeser, napkin-doodling colleague from Wisconsin's CESA 6, for his initial draft of the five critical questions

Colleagues and contributors in the Seattle School District: Eric Benson, Charlotte Carr, Wendy Cornacchio, Gary Cranston, Joan Dore, Jane Goetz, Joani Harr, Allison Harris, Stephanie Haskins, John Humphrie, Cothron L. McMillian-Dickey, Mike O'Connell, Joanne Testacross, and Rosalind Wise

Colorado's Cindy Harrison and Jan Herrera, and Wisconsin's Blane McCann, Jim Fergus, and Terri Huck

And to many more dedicated educators in Arizona, Arkansas, Colorado, Florida, Indiana, Iowa, Kentucky, Louisiana, Michigan, New Jersey, New York, Ohio, Oregon, South Carolina, Texas, Virginia, Wisconsin, Guam, Canada, St. Lucia, and Hong Kong, whose work to improve their schools provides examples for this book and for the professional lives of all of us.

About the Author

Edie L. Holcomb is highly regarded for her ability to link research and practice on issues related to school leadership, improvement, and reform. She holds a BS in elementary education, an MS in gifted education, and an EdS in educational administration. She received her PhD in educational administration from the University of Minnesota. Her background includes teaching experience at all grade levels and administrative experience at the building and district level in Illinois, Alabama, Minnesota, South Dakota, Iowa, and Wisconsin. She served as Associate Director of the National Center for Effective Schools, developing *School-Based Instructional Leadership*, a training program for site-based teams. She has provided technical assistance for implementation of school improvement efforts throughout the United States and in Canada, Guam, St. Lucia, and Hong Kong. Her recent work has included synthesizing change efforts such as outcome-based education and total quality management with existing school improvement frameworks. As Associate Professor of Educational Administration at Wichita State University in Kansas, she coordinated the principalship course and internships and taught applied inquiry in the field-based doctoral program. She now serves the 47,000 students and 5,000 staff of the Seattle School District as Director of Standards and Assessment.

1

Introduction

Why does the phone ring only when something's on the stove, my hands are in the sink, my body's in the bathtub, or my mind is in some other state? This time when it jangled, my wet body was in Wisconsin while my mind was in Michigan grappling with the needs of my recently widowed mom and trying to fast-forward myself through the stages of grief. An unfamiliar voice on the other end asked, "Is this the Edie Holcomb who's been consulting with the Restructuring Committee?" As I acknowledged that identity, mental red lights and alarm bells kicked in full force. Reporter? Board member? Misinformed nonparticipant? "Well, my name is John Doe.[1] I'm on the scheduling committee at our high school, and we've been studying a four-period day, and that's what we want to recommend to the whole faculty. But there's going to be a lot of resistance, and I was told you know a lot of group processes, and I'm wondering if you could recommend the approach that would work best." The relief that it wasn't the media was followed by sheer panic as my mental screen went absolutely blank, and I asked myself: "If I'm the Edie Holcomb who knows a lot of group process techniques, why can't I think of a single one right now? I need a 'crib sheet' to hang by every phone in my house and office so I can *remember* what I know when I get these unexpected phone calls!"

A few days later, body clothed but mind in a state of frustration, I looked around a large square of tables at a room full of staff developers from intermediate and state education agencies. I had been hired by this group for three purposes: to present the effective schools research as a knowledge base, then introduce and apply findings on school change processes, and finally integrate components of the state's approach to Goals 2000 and other state standards. These outcomes were to be achieved in three once-a-month workshops. Only one had occurred so far.

The planning session had deteriorated into a defense of each agency's preferred model for school change as most current, most comprehensive, and most worthy of becoming a statewide model. Sincere, conscientious professionals who had spent the coffee break bemoaning the difficulties of breaking down departmental barriers in high schools were engaged in their own turf wars, talking at cross-purposes about the same concepts, each armed with his or her particular guru's customized vocabulary. This time I asked myself, "Why is this happening, even in a group that knows better? What we need is a set of factors that are common to all these processes, use no educational jargon, and have no capital letters to turn into acronyms!"

Scenario 3

Coffee cups and cookie crumbs littered the table as the apprehensive group of principals wrestled with the role changes occurring as a result of the district's mandate for site-based management. Official job descriptions and evaluation systems remained unchanged, but every building was to form a school council, and the administrators would be held responsible for its success. Even those most optimistic, cheering up the others with the potential for greater autonomy and authentic shared decision making, wondered whether they had the knowledge and skills to pull it off. One voice rose above the rest. "I'm supposed to form a team, and I don't even know who should be on it or what it should do. No one in my school— not even me—has ever been to a workshop on teamwork. We need some training first, but we have to start without it. What we need is an outline of the things we'll need to know and which ones come first, so we can learn as we go."

Synthesis

Some wise—or at least widely quoted—person said that important things come in threes. True or not, the aphorism applies because these three episodes happened within the space of a few weeks and resulted in the matrix around which this book has developed (see Figure 1.1).

The row of group process techniques across the top is a sideways version of the list I developed as my own skill catalog from which to select, modify, and/or combine tried-and-true methods when presented with a new consulting question or facilitating challenge. Development of the five questions in the left-hand column began in Scenario 2 and is described in more detail in Chapter 2. Each of Chapters 3 through 7 provides directions for use of group processes and describes their application in examples from real school experiences. There are other group processes that work very well, and there are additional ways to use those included here. I am simply sharing the techniques I know, as I've used them, and the settings in which I have been able to help others apply them successfully. Uses of the matrix to assist others such as the struggling principals of Scenario 3 are outlined in Chapter 9.

(text continues on page 6)

FIGURE 1.1. Matrix of Tools for Asking the Right Questions

Where Are We Now? (readiness, planning, and training,[a] initiation[b])	Think, Pair, Share	Flowcharting	Pareto Charts	Pie Charts	Histograms	Run Charts	Surveys	Focus Groups	Affinity Process	Brainstorming	Nominal Group Process	Color Coding	Weighted Voting	Fishbone (Cause and Effect)	Force Field Analysis	Decision Matrix	Action Planning	CBAM-SoCQ	Quick-Write	Venn Diagram	Go for the Green	TalkWalk	Action Research	Reflective Study Groups	Active Listening	Networking	Continuum	Graphic Organizer
Raise awareness of need for change	3	X						X	X	X		X		X					X	X		X		X	X			
Clarify roles and responsibilities	X	X						X	X	X		X							X	X	X				X	X	3	X
Diagnose motivation for change (source, intensity)	X						X	X	X									X	X	X					X		X	
Review existing philosophy, mission, belief statements	X						X	X	X			X	X	X					X	X				X	X			
Diagnose governance and program factors	X	3	X				X	X	X			X		X				X	X	X			X		X			X
Diagnose student success				3	3	3	X	X						X									X	X	X			
Diagnose shareholder perceptions			X	X	X		3	X	X			X	X	X	X				X	X			X	X	X			
Diagnose organizational culture, climate	X		X				X	3		X		X		X				X	X	X	X		X		X	X	X	X

(continued)

3

FIGURE 1.1. Continued

	Think, Pair, Share	Flowcharting	Pareto Charts	Pie Charts	Histograms	Run Charts	Surveys	Focus Groups	Affinity Process	Brainstorming	Nominal Group Process	Color Coding	Weighted Voting	Fishbone (Cause and Effect)	Force Field Analysis	Decision Matrix	Action Planning	CBAM-SoCQ	Quick-Write	Venn Diagram	Go for the Green	TalkWalk	Action Research	Reflective Study Groups	Active Listening	Networking	Continuum	Graphic Organizer
Where Do We Want to Go? (planning and training;[a] initiation;[b] plan[c])																												
Develop/affirm mission statement	X						X	X	4	X		X							X						X			X
Stimulate visioning	X							X	X	4															X			
Prioritize concerns			X		X		X			X	4	4	4		X	X			X						X			
Set goals/targets with focus on students	X										X													X				
Identify best practices															X	X							X	X				X
How Will We Get There? (planning, training, and implementation;[a] implementation;[b] plan[c])																												
Identify factors related to concerns	X	5	5		X		X	X	X	X	X	X		5	X				X		X	X	X	X	X			
Identify barriers	X	X						X	X	X	X	X		X	5				X		X	X	X	X	X			
Select strategies								X	X		X	X		5	5							X	X	X	X			5
Develop action plans	X															5					X							
Identify indicators/data to monitor	X								X	X	X	X						X					X		X	X	X	X
Affirm mission and beliefs	X						X	X	X	X	X	X						X			X			X	X	X	X	X

How Will We Know We Are (Getting) There?
(implementation and maintenance;[a] implementation;[b] do and check[c])

Item														
Monitor progress on identified indicators/data		X	X	X				X						
Affirm mission and beliefs	X			X	X	X	X		X		X	X	X	
Identify and respond to individuals' concerns	X			X	X	X	X	7	X	X	X	X	X	X

How Will We Sustain the Focus and Momentum?
(maintenance;[a] institutionalization;[b] check, act, and plan[c])

Item														
Cope with conflict							7	7	7		7		X	X
Build culture of inquiry										7	X	X	X	X
Monitor progress and adjust strategies	X	X	X	X	X	X	X	X		X	X	X	X	
Affirm mission and beliefs	X			X	X	X		X		X		7	X	X
Support leaders and followers	X			X	X	X	X	X		X	X	X	7	X

NOTE: Numbers in cells indicate the chapter in which the topic is covered.
a. From the RPTIM model (readiness, planning, training, implementation, and maintenance). See p. 9.
b. From the Three Is model (initiation, implementation, and institutionalization). See p. 9.
c. From the PDCA cycle (plan-do-check-act). See p. 10.

This book does not pretend to contribute a vast depository of new knowledge to the field of organizational development and school change. That knowledge is already available, and some helpful sources are listed in the annotated bibliography. What this book adds is practical tips and stories of application and implementation from educational settings. If *Asking the Right Questions: Techniques for Collaboration and School Change* finds a unique niche, it will be as a synthesizer of skills often learned in isolated fragments and of processes that now compete for the "one best way" award. It is neither a scholarly tome on change research nor an exhaustive compendium of detailed exercises defended with academic rationale. The annotated bibliography is provided to assist the reader with those needs. This is simply a "what can I do with my group on Monday with the skills I already have" guide for leaders of school-based teams, whether laypersons or experienced educators.

Note

1. Some schools and individuals in this book are not identified to preserve their potential for growth.

2

Asking the Right Questions

The tension continued into lunchtime. The moderator of the meeting, an administrator with outstanding facilitation skills but limited history with the group, expressed a sense of failure with the lack of progress and a desire to go back to his office where he could accomplish something. The suspiciously convenient ringing of his cell phone granted that wish. By this time, doubting *anyone's* ability to meet the varied expectations of the group, I offered to withdraw and let the group clarify what it really wanted and determine whether another presenter would be more suitable for the two remaining sessions. One agency's representative actually asked for her handouts back and went home. But one dedicated member of the group sat thoughtfully, apparently doodling on his napkin.

When the group reconvened, colleague Dennis Glaeser volunteered his napkin notes, five questions that reflected the themes evolving during the discussion of change models. The questions were as follows:

- ◆ Where are we now?
- ◆ Where do we want to go?
- ◆ How will we get there?
- ◆ How will we know we are there?
- ◆ How can we keep it going?

This set of questions broke the gridlock, and the remaining participants began to link their desired topics to the five headings. As the content agenda developed, the original direction to ground the workshops in the knowledge base of effective schools research was restated. This focus on findings from school settings created a common ground with ideas originating in business and industry.

Refinement of the Five Critical Questions

The questions generated that day reminded me of the question-answer format used by Larry Lezotte and Barbara Jacoby in their *Guide to the School Improvement Process Based on Effective Schools Research.*

Lezotte and Jacoby described the school improvement process in five stages: preparation, focus, diagnosis, plan development, and implementation/monitoring. Their guiding question for the focus stage was "Where do we want to go?" The diagnosis stage included interpretation of student outcomes and organizational dimensions in response to the question "How are we doing?" Plan development resulted from consideration of "How will we get to where we want to go?" And their stage of implementation, monitoring, evaluation, and renewal was prompted by the query "How will we know we got there?"

In addition to the reinforcement provided by Lezotte and Jacoby, the guiding questions used in this book were also influenced by the work of Michael Fullan and others who have written about change in organizations. Writers on school change speak of 3 to 5 years for a moderately complex change and 5 to 7 years for major restructuring to move from being an innovation to becoming a routine part of how the organization conducts its primary functions. In a recent presentation,[1] Fullan introduced the new "3-6-8 rule." On the basis of his research and experience, he has concluded that an elementary school can make significant change in *three* years, but it takes *six* years to change a high school and *eight* years to transform an entire school district.

With those time frames in mind, asking "How will we know we are there?" seemed inappropriate. Such a question implies that monitoring is exclusively summative, occurring at some distant point of completion in the future. In a society programmed for immediate gratification, motivation based on proof of successful results would be difficult with such a long lag time. The question "How will we know we are there?" thus became "How will we know we are (getting) there?" The added word in parentheses reminds us of the need for milestones or benchmarks that will verify gradual progress and reinforce continued effort.

Literature on stages of change also influenced the last question, which now reads "How will we sustain the focus and momentum?" One of the most common problems faced by change agents in schools is the TYNT-NYNT syndrome: "this year's new thing" soon replaced by "next year's new thing." Fullan, Miles, Huberman, and others have pointed out the need to continue a change process from initiation to implementation and on to institutionalization. The "bandwagon" approach so common to school change efforts prevents this sustained momentum. At the same time, Elmore and others have pointed out that the time and effort it takes to restructure schools are not warranted unless they directly affect the aspects of teaching that improve student learning. The importance of maintaining focus on student outcomes, as well as the momentum of energy and resources, is reflected in the wording of the fifth question: "How will we sustain the focus and momentum?"

The Five Questions and Three Models of Change

In response to the needs expressed in the three scenarios of Chapter 1, these five critical questions were used as the five major sections of a matrix (Figure 1.1) for matching group process skills with aspects of school improvement efforts. These five sections are also headed by terminology from three well-known models, processes, or descriptions of change.

RPTIM

The first is Wood's RPTIM model, a classic from staff development literature. The acronym stands for stages of readiness, planning, training, implementation, and maintenance. The **readiness** stage includes identifying major problems of the school or district, working in collaboration with key groups to develop goals, and examining current practices. The **planning** stage includes identifying differences between goals, desired practices, and actual practices and planning training activities based on that diagnosis. During the **training** stage, all affected groups including central office administrators, principals, teachers, and others receive training and develop, share, and critique action plans. **Implementation** requires that resources are allocated to support new practices and that additional coaching and training are provided on a continuing basis. The **maintenance** stage involves supervision and monitoring to continue new behaviors and use of feedback to guide further improvement. Although Wood's work focused specifically on staff development and instructional changes, his framework has been generalized by school districts and regional labs to guide many effective schools projects.

The Three *I*s

A second well-known description of change is presented in writings by Miles, Huberman, and Fullan and is often referred to as the Three *I*s: initiation, implementation, and institutionalization. A key factor in the **initiation** of change is identification of a high-profile need that participants feel is relevant to them, for which a sense of readiness has been created, and for which resources have been allocated to demonstrate the organization's commitment. The visibility of a few strong advocates who can present a clear model of implementation and actively move it forward is an essential aspect of successful initiation.

The **implementation** stage requires attention to unique local characteristics of the community, district, and its principals and teachers. Overall coordination is needed but must be balanced by shared control, which I refer to here as shared leadership. The balancing of pressure and support through communication of clear expectations for progress and improvement, while providing technical assistance and rewards, is critical. Fullan's description of essentials for implementation includes vision building, initiative taking, staff training, monitoring, and evolutionary planning—with continual adjustment as data and feedback are received and analyzed.

Many change processes survive through initiation, and attempts are made to implement them, but they do not take root and do not become embedded in the culture. Among the reasons that this **institutionalization** does not occur are lack of close links to the teaching and learning process and lack of continued training and support until new practices are in widespread use. Sustaining focus and momentum requires continued assistance with new practices and removal of competing priorities.

PDCA

Other descriptions of organizational change and improvement have emerged from the business sector, especially the total quality management literature. A model that has been applied in schools is the plan-do-check-act (PDCA) cycle. The **plan** stage involves identifying a needed change, assembling available data and collecting new data to clarify what needs to occur, and identifying root causes of the problem. To **do** means to generate possible solutions, select and implement them on a pilot basis, and gather data on the results. A **check** verifies what has been accomplished, confirms what worked well and what did not, and analyzes results before implementing an attempted solution on a broader scale. Decisions are made to **act** on the results by either abandoning the new practice or standardizing it to ensure consistency throughout the organization. Processes are continually monitored, and the cycle is repeated.

In Figure 1.1, the five guiding questions were used to cross-walk these models of change and identify group process activities for involving shareholders. But by the time the first edition of *Asking the Right Questions* went to press, more questions were emerging.

Scenario 4

As part of Kentucky's education reform agenda, leadership teams throughout the state received training in effective schools research and the school improvement process. Materials from the *School-Based Instructional Leadership* training program that I developed at the National Center for Effective Schools were used as a resource, and I was one of the consultants involved in the training design and delivery. Two years later, after *Asking the Right Questions* was published, it was used in follow-up visits with a state cadre of facilitators. Several participants commented on the frequent references to data throughout the book. One of them told me, "This is much more than a book on teamwork. It's really a 'data book.' State assessment and accountability systems are requiring so much more attention to results, and grants for continued funding keep demanding more documentation. We need you to pull the data pieces out and write more about them."

Getting Excited About Data: How to Combine People, Passion, and Proof was the response to that request. As the title implies, the specific focus of that book is not only that data should be used but that people need to be engaged with the data and with each other and need to see and feel connections between the "hard numbers" and their passion for students and learning. *Getting Excited About Data* is not a technical statistics book but rather a "consumer report" about how to use data. It explores the reasons why teachers are reluctant to work with data and offers ideas for overcoming that resistance.

The two books reinforce each other. Many of the process skills described in the first edition of this book were adapted into data-related group activities for *Getting Excited*. Figure 2.1 was developed as a graphic organizer for that book, and a more detailed explanation of the component parts, their relationships, and the uses of data can be found there.

For this edition, Figure 2.1 has been further clarified with the addition of the five guiding questions. The overview at the end of this chapter outlines the connections between the models of change and this graphic organizer. This section

FIGURE 2.1. School Change as Inquiry

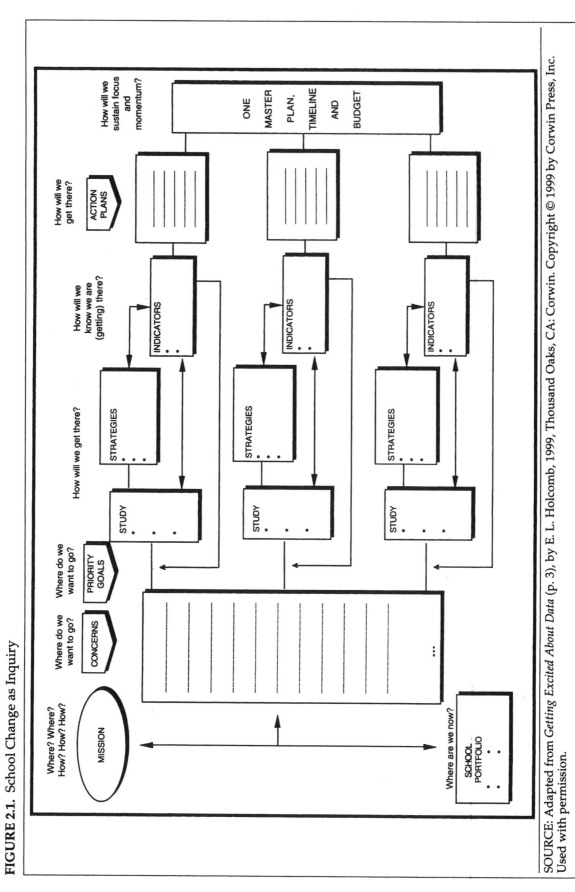

SOURCE: Adapted from *Getting Excited About Data* (p. 3), by E. L. Holcomb, 1999, Thousand Oaks, CA: Corwin. Copyright © 1999 by Corwin Press, Inc. Used with permission.

provides a quick walk through the various components of school improvement as an inquiry process.

Developing a **portfolio** of information about the school is part of identifying "where we are now." Developing, or reviewing and affirming, our **mission** and core values begins the dialogue about "where we want to go." The two-sided arrow between mission and the evidence in our portfolio illustrates that the distance between what we *believe* and what we really *achieve* may be long or short. The greater the discrepancy between our mission and our results, the longer will be our list of **concerns.** From these, we must carefully select a limited number of **priority goals.** These goals further define "where we want to go."

Once goals are set, collaborative groups undertake the **study** process that will lead to decisions about the **strategies** that represent "how we will get there" and the **indicators** that will be monitored so we will "know we are (getting) there." The three bullets in the "Study" box represent different approaches. One is to review the research on effective practices that address the goal. Another is to consult with other schools, districts, and education agencies that face similar challenges and identify their successes as best practice. The third is to further analyze the available data, and perhaps collect more, to better understand the challenge and identify the barriers that must be overcome.

The multiple points in the "Strategies" box are less specific. There is no specific meaning for each one, as outlined for the three aspects of "study." Instead, these multiple points remind us that there is no single "one best way" that will guarantee success in reaching a goal. For example, increasing reading achievement may require a simultaneous combination of strategies, such as

◆ Changing curriculum materials

◆ Learning new teaching strategies

◆ Revising the school schedule to allow for more flexible grouping and lower student-adult ratios

◆ Devising ways to attract and involve more parents/guardians in their children's education

The two points in the box labeled "Indicators" represent two types of criteria that should be identified at the outset. The most obvious is the outcome indicators that will document the desired results. In the above example, the outcome indicators (or **indicators of impact**) would be measures of reading achievement that show that students are really learning more since those changes have been initiated. The other point in the "Indicators" box represents **indicators of implementation.** These are the criteria that are established to show that the new strategies are actually being used. They might include documents, such as the new school schedule and logs of parent activity, or observational comments made by the principal or peer coaches about new teaching strategies.

The two-way arrow between "Strategies" and "Indicators" illustrates that this is not a purely linear relationship. Sometimes groups have to think about how the desired situation would look, and what evidence they would need to gather, to have greater clarity about the changes in practice that are required. The arrow from "Indicators" back to "Study" creates a cycle within a cycle. If research-based strategies are faithfully implemented but the indicators do not yield evidence of improved results, further study and modified strategies will be needed.

Answering the "how will we get there?" question also requires development of **action plans** that clarify roles, responsibilities, timelines, and resources needed for implementation. The ability to "sustain focus and momentum" is greatly increased when these action plans are then coordinated as components of one **master plan.** Without this step, it is impossible to get a systemic picture of all the activity being attempted within a school. When the action plans are reviewed, competing demands for financial resources and professional development time become clear and can be adjusted so that the school's efforts are cohesive, rather than fragmented, and can be conducted in a coordinated manner.

Scenario 5

She is one of those tall, slender redheads with emerald green eyes that you'd expect to encounter in a movie or romance novel. The stereotypical male lead would be astounded to learn that she's the mother of teenagers, a teacher, a doctoral candidate, and a curriculum leader in one of the consortium districts described in *Getting Excited About Data.* After participating in a series of training sessions on school improvement, I was the one stunned to see her eyes swimming with blinked-back tears as she challenged me with this question: "The *state* has been hitting us with standards and assessments and test data and accountability goals. So we've been spending hours and hours and all our staff development money at the *district* getting our curriculum aligned and checking our course outlines and writing performance assessments to be sure our students are ready. Now you're just talking about *school* improvement and how real change has to happen at the *school* level. Are you saying we've spent the last 2 years doing the wrong things? What about all our hard work already?"

Her sincere, anguished question cut right through me as I recognized my teaching error. By what I had left unsaid, I had conveyed the impression of an either/or relationship between school and district leadership in change. The truth is that both are essential. Too much emphasis on either the school or district is problematic, and lack of clarity about "who does what" is one of the biggest barriers to forward movement and systemic thinking.

In *Change Forces: The Sequel,* Michael Fullan talks about the ill effects of both ends of the pendulum swing in the Chicago school reform movement. In the 1980s, schools in Chicago were virtually paralyzed by the excessive bureaucracy emanating from the district offices. Then in 1988, the system went to the other extreme, decentralized with local school councils hiring and firing their principals. After 6 years with little contact occurring between schools and the district, the system was "recentered" in 1994. Many aspects of decentralization remain, but new functions of central support, capacity building, and accountability have emerged.

Questions about school and district roles, such as those raised in Scenario 5, are addressed in Chapter 3. For this edition, new material has been added about site-based management, along with tools to use in defining roles and relationships, so that the school can operate effectively within its organizational context.

A new section has also been added to Chapter 5, which explores the question of "How will we get there?" Figure 5.8 is a flowchart that starts from the point where student performance needs are identified. Posing a series of questions about why students may not be achieving, it illustrates the difference in how the district and school respond to those questions.

Still More Questions: An Overview

Why is the school change process like a two-year-old? Some might say it's because "no one likes change except a wet baby." That may be true—but most two-year-olds have achieved a level of self-actualization that eliminates the need for an "external change agent." School change is like a two-year-old in the respect that one question leads inexorably to another. The two-year-old's questions start with "whatzat" and proceed through multiple "why's." Our guiding questions begin with "where" and "how," but the embedded "why's" are inescapable. They surface regularly and are an important reminder of the critical need for continuing collaboration.

This section provides an overview of each of the remaining chapters, connects it to the matrix in Figure 1.1 and the graphic organizer in Figure 2.1, and highlights new material in this second edition.

Chapter 3: Where Are We Now?

Chapter 3 provides discussion of the factors to consider in addressing the "where are we now?" question. Under this heading in Figure 1.1 are references to the readiness, planning, and training stages of Wood's RPTIM model and the initiation stage of the Three Is model.

On Figure 2.1, the "where are we now?" question is posed above the area called "School Portfolio." This represents the collection of all the information listed above. The oval labeled "Mission" is the only oval on the page and has the first word of all five questions posed above it. The unique shape and the reference to all five questions are visual reminders that the core values of the school must be continuously and consciously introduced in all discussion of all decisions in a change process. (Chapter 4 includes a group process activity that helps an organization articulate its core values.)

Chapter 3 includes three main sections. The first two describe ways to use data on student achievement and perceptual data that communicate a sense of "customer satisfaction" with the school.

A third section addresses the need to clarify roles and responsibilities within the organizational culture and context. Within the school, a leadership group needs to coordinate the work of subcommittees or task forces and needs skills to facilitate engagement of the entire staff at major decision points. But the school does not operate in a void, and the clarification of roles and relationships with the school district and community is also essential.

In the first edition, I used the term *stakeholders* to describe individuals and groups who have a stake in the outcome of decisions about their school. Here I use the preferred term *shareholders*, hoping that it more accurately conveys not only interest in the results but also a share in the planning and an acceptance of shared responsibility for accomplishment.

Parents are certainly major shareholders, but other *external* shareholders must be considered as well because parents represent a declining segment of the taxpayers who support the schools. The term *community* is used here in a broader way to include social service agencies, businesses, and taxpayers who do not have children attending school. There are also *internal* shareholders, because every employee of the district—administrator, teacher, social and health worker, clerical employee, custodian, food and transportation provider—is affected by how the organization functions. The interactions between and among these groups establish the culture of the organization and enhance or inhibit accomplishment of its mission and goals for students.

New material in Chapter 3 includes a section on constructing a continuum to define roles and responsibilities in site-based management. The story of Thornton High School tells how a school rebuilt its governance structure to renew its sense of mission and focus on schoolwide goals.

Chapter 4: Where Do We Want to Go?

As shown in Figure 1.1, the question of "Where do we want to go?" encompasses the planning and training stages of the RPTIM model, more of the initiation stage of the Three *Is*, and the plan tasks of PDCA. At this stage, mission statements are written or clarified, and belief statements are affirmed and used to ground the selection of goals.

Figure 2.1 shows how the question of "where to go" is linked to the school's mission and how the long list of concerns about a school is narrowed to a few priority goals. Group process activities are provided to guide goal setting.

Chapter 5: How Will We Get There?

Goals turn into action plans as colleagues in schools address the question "How will we get there?" This stage spans planning, training, and implementation from all three models of change (see Figure 1.1). Major tasks are represented by the "Study" and "Strategies" sections of Figure 2.1, described earlier in this chapter. One reason that school improvement efforts fail is that too many schools leap into planning without devoting adequate time to analyzing their own issues internally and learning from others outside the school. Chapter 5 introduces three new questions that slow down the brainstorming for more in-depth analysis of their problems, study of research findings about their priority goal areas, and exploration of best practices being used successfully by other schools. Figure 5.8 is introduced as a way to link district and school discussions specifically about issues of student performance.

Chapter 6: How Will We Know We Are (Getting) There?

Answering the question "How will we know we are (getting) there?" stimulates a renewed focus on the desired outcomes of change. Figure 1.1 demonstrates how this question includes the stages of implementation, maintenance, and monitoring from the RPTIM model, continues the implementation described in the Three *Is*, and moves to the do and check steps of PDCA.

On Figure 2.1, the guiding question about how we'll know we're getting there is posed above the "Indicators" section. Two points emphasize the need for indicators that the planned strategies are being implemented, as well as indicators of their impact on students. The two-way arrows from "Indicators" to "Strategies" and back to "Study" and even back to "Priority Goals" show the importance of this work because of its potential to guide adjustments in strategies, elicit needs for further study, and even clarify the intended goals and enlighten future goal setting.

Visible results of a school's efforts provide both the carrot and the stick to sustain the difficult effort of school change. Success breeds success, and evidence of progress motivates sustained effort. Regular monitoring of key indicators conveys a strong message that change is an expectation. Chapter 6 now includes the evaluation plan developed at John Bullen Middle School to coordinate its change efforts, document implementation of its comprehensive school reform design, and provide information to staff and community. The Nathan Hale High School story is added as an example of how careful study of principles and beliefs led to specific plans and documented results for students.

Chapter 7: How Will We Sustain Focus and Momentum?

The most complex of the five guiding questions is this: How will we sustain focus and momentum? So many new efforts start out with enthusiasm and show great promise but somehow evaporate before really delivering on their potential. As Figure 1.1 demonstrates, attention must be given to the critical elements of maintenance, institutionalization, and the PDCA tasks of check, act, and *adjust* plan. The comprehensive, coordinated school plan shown in Figure 2.1 can help keep a change effort on track. The five questions poised above "Mission" also remind us that it takes constant vigilance to keep an organization on the high road of operating in ways that are consistent with its values.

The need for monitoring outlined in Chapter 6 continues, but a shift must occur to make the need and motivation for change more internal. Techniques such as reflective study groups and action research engage participants through their own interest areas. True courage is needed to identify and abandon nonproductive practices. At the same time, relationships between and among groups and participants must be maintained and strengthened through problem solving and conflict resolution. Chapter 7 also includes tips on how to dedicate time for collaboration. New questions are presented that help schools evaluate opportunities as they occur and make decisions about what to integrate and what to ignore. The story of Rainier View Elementary School is shared as an illustration of maintaining momentum by celebrating progress toward their goals.

Chapter 8: Bonus Questions

Chapter 7 concludes the walk through the school improvement process. Chapter 8 raises several questions for further thought. When faced with deeply held beliefs and traditions, educators must ask, "Did it make sense then?" and "Does it make sense now?" While learning to increase collaboration and shareholder engagement, we learn to ask, "Who else should be included?" When tempted to give up, we must reflect on the question "Who else, if not me?"

Chapter 9: Using This Book

Chapter 9 concludes with recommendations for applying Figures 1.1 and 2.1 and the group process activities in this book to your personal professional growth and your organization. The book can be a guide for team training, coaching new facilitators, and analyzing processes and plans. The story of Madison Middle School illustrates the interrelationship of all systems and their impact on student performance.

Note

1. "Change Forces at the Millennium," National Staff Development Council Annual Conference, Dallas, Texas, December 6, 1999.

3

Answering the "Where Are We Now?" Question

"The journey of a thousand miles begins with a single step." If school change is a journey, then colleagues and shareholders are the travelers. But some are serious explorers, and others are only ramblers. Travelers follow their maps; ramblers follow their noses. Travelers have a destination in mind, and they lay out a route from here to there. Knowing the starting point is just as important as knowing the destination if the journey is to be safe, accurate, timely, and cost-effective. Travelers also check weather conditions, make lists, and assemble needed items. In short, ramblers say "Let's go somewhere." Travelers say, "Let's gather some information, make a plan, and *then* go."

The journey of school change is never an easy one, and there are many hazards along the way, but the trip can get off to its smoothest start by carefully analyzing the present situation. This chapter includes tips and techniques for addressing the question "Where are we now?" (see Figures 1.1 and 2.1.). Three critical aspects of the school's or district's status must be analyzed: student performance, shareholder perceptions, and organizational culture and context.

When we think of data on **student performance,** our instinctive response is to visualize graphs of test scores and leave it at that. This initial limited scope implies that acquisition of discrete bits of knowledge is the sole and complete function of the school and gives the test makers more credit than they deserve. If a school or district justifies its test results with claims that "these tests don't cover all the things we try to accomplish in school," that organization must identify ways to demonstrate that it does accomplish all those other things. Desirable student results such as citizenship are more clearly revealed in data such as attendance, participation in service activities, and occurrences of vandalism and disruptive behavior.

Schools and districts must acknowledge the reality that public education is a service industry that must be user friendly or lose its "market share" to vouchers, private schools, and for-profit enterprises. Surveys, telephone interviews, and focus groups are among the methods often used to gather **shareholder perceptions.**

Gathering the information, however, is only the first step and can do more harm than good if not followed by analyzing, interpreting, and reporting the results back to the constituents and using the data in goal setting and planning for improvement.

The school **culture and context** include roles and relationships, the history of and motivation for prior change in the organization, and an awareness of governance and program factors that may inhibit or enhance new efforts. Only through sensitivity to the past can change agents link innovation with events remembered fondly and disassociate new practices from those that have left bitter legacies.

Site-based management is a significant aspect of the organizational context that must be addressed in this stage. Too little autonomy at the school level inhibits the leadership team's ability to build credibility and commitment for the change process through authentic decision making. Too much autonomy leaves the school in the position of navigating a river without knowing where the banks are. Immense amounts of energy can be expended "reinventing wheels" that could be provided at scale with district support. Lack of communication and clarification about the definition of site-based management in the local setting can create confusion, chaos, and frustration.

This chapter describes group processes that can be employed to help a school or district ask itself, "Where are we now?" Each description includes the purpose of the group technique, appropriate timing, recommended participants, materials needed, and tips to guide the facilitator.

A new section describes ways of clarifying roles and relationships, and the story of Thornton High School illustrates how a staff worked together to restructure a "stuck" process.

Student Performance

Every school improvement effort I have encountered has espoused "increased student achievement" as its foundation. Given that commonality, I have been amazed at the number of school improvement plans that include no references to student performance or goals that relate to the process of teaching and learning. When most districts report on student performance, they use a mean (average) score based on aggregate (all scores mixed together) data. This type of reporting has contributed to myths such as the "Lake Wobegon effect" that "all the children are above average." Schools and districts with homogeneous populations and a strong cultural work ethic are lulled into complacency by mean scores that rank favorably with schools and districts facing far greater challenges.

Histograms

Use of a histogram to depict student performance can provide more accurate information and a better analysis of the current performance level of students and the school's success at teaching.

Purpose. A histogram is a type of bar chart or graph that shows a distribution of information. It allows educators to see the range and variation in student achievement, rather than an overall average score. This provides a much better picture of how well the school is fulfilling its obligation to teach all children.

When to Use. An examination of current student performance should be one of the early steps in addressing the "Where are we now?" question. The same analysis should be conducted each time a general assessment is used, and each set of results should be added to the longitudinal trend data being accumulated.

Whom to Involve. School psychologists and counselors are valuable members of a work group that is compiling data on student achievement and behavior. The group should also include teachers who work with the student population in the subject areas (of a cognitive assessment) or in the school environment (in case of behavior). Although test data may initially be compiled by specialists such as the testing companies or school district research and evaluation departments, interpretation of what the data mean should be done in concert with the teachers who work with the students on a daily basis. It is difficult to engage teachers in the use of data, especially if they are demeaned by having data returned to them with weak areas or low scores already highlighted as if they can't make those distinctions themselves. (Chapter 3 of *Getting Excited About Data* is devoted to the reasons why teachers are reluctant to engage with data and suggests strategies for building comfort and confidence.)

Materials Needed. A histogram can be constructed to represent any type of data available and relevant for discussion, for example, test scores, grades, attendance, and discipline referrals. A laptop computer and appropriate software can make the job easier, but there is learning value in having groups do rough drafts of their histograms on paper.

Tips for Facilitators

The first step is to create a frequency distribution of the scores, number of absences, or other factors to be analyzed. The second step is to divide the full range of scores into a usable number of categories or classes. In the case of norm-referenced achievement scores, testing companies often array the scores in stanines. Another good set of categories for examining student performance is the use of quartiles. This divides scores into those that fall between the 1st and 25th percentiles, 26th and 50th percentiles, 51st and 75th, and 76th percentile and above. A histogram with one high bar in the third quartile may verify that a commendable mean of 70th percentile really represents success of all students. A histogram with a high bar in the third or fourth quartile but also in the lowest quartile can indicate that there are enough high-achieving students to influence the mean and mask the reality that the school is not meeting its obligation to another segment of its population. Many new state assessments report scores in levels of proficiency, so each bar on a histogram would represent the number of students in Level 1, Level 2, and so on.

For Example: Quartiles

Figure 3.1 is actually a combination of eight histograms. The math scores for each grade level are represented in quartiles. It takes only a glance to discover that the distribution of performance provides a lot more information than a mean score for the entire grade. Graphic displays such as the histogram provide information but are even more powerful in prompting further questions. Groups should be

20

FIGURE 3.1. Histogram of Student Achievement

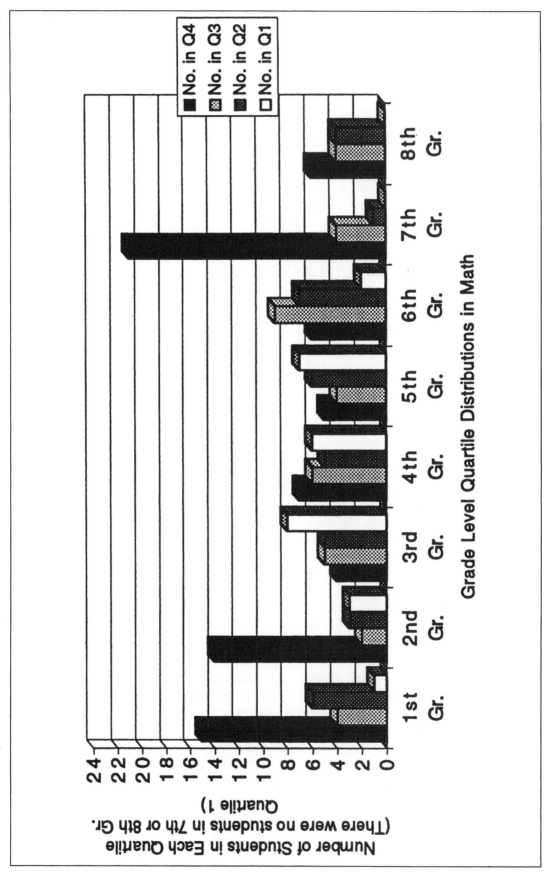

challenged to discuss the following questions: What else might this tell us? What do we do with this information? and What do we want these histograms to look like 3 years from now? The last question is particularly important if a school has not used data in the past and has only the "snapshot" data of the current year to use as a baseline.

A Variation: Disaggregation

The histogram is introduced in this chapter as one example of how graphs can display data in ways that are understandable and that prompt further examination of student learning. Many schools with heterogeneous populations have made commitments to equity and want to know whether the distribution of performance is the same for all groups within the total student population. Factors such as race/ethnicity and socioeconomic status (SES) are often considered. In Figure 3.2, the performance scores have been separated to compare the distribution of scores for students from low-SES homes with those from more affluent settings. This display is also called a *stacked bar graph* because the distribution is shown as boxes "stacked" within each bar.

The process of breaking up data to examine the performance of different subgroups is called *disaggregation*. Although this histogram shows that 63% of all students rank in the top two quartiles, it also points out that only 37% and 39% of the students from minority groups achieve at this level.

Another Twist: Student Performance

The term *student performance* can encompass more than academic success. Schools often have other expectations that relate to goals such as good citizenship. These schools may use data such as attendance, punctuality, completion of assignments, participation in service projects, behavior, and vandalism to assess how well the school is helping students develop characteristics of good citizenship. Such data can also be displayed in histograms to help a school ask itself, "Where are we now in student performance?"

Run Charts

The histogram, pie chart (see Chapter 5), and most other graphs represent information at a certain point in time. In contrast, the run chart can illustrate trends in data over a span of time.

Purpose. The run chart monitors a situation or process through time to identify changes. Although the histograms in Figure 3.3 show distribution of student achievement on one year's scores, a run chart shows how those same students score from one year to the next and whether their achievement improves, declines, or stays the same.

When to Use. If a school or district has been collecting data over time, a run chart can be constructed in the early stages of addressing the "Where are we now?" question. Sometimes schools have not used test scores or other data in any systematic way, but they can go back and re-create a run chart to show a history of what has been occurring. In other cases, schools can only gather data for the first

FIGURE 3.2. Histogram of Disaggregated Student Achievement

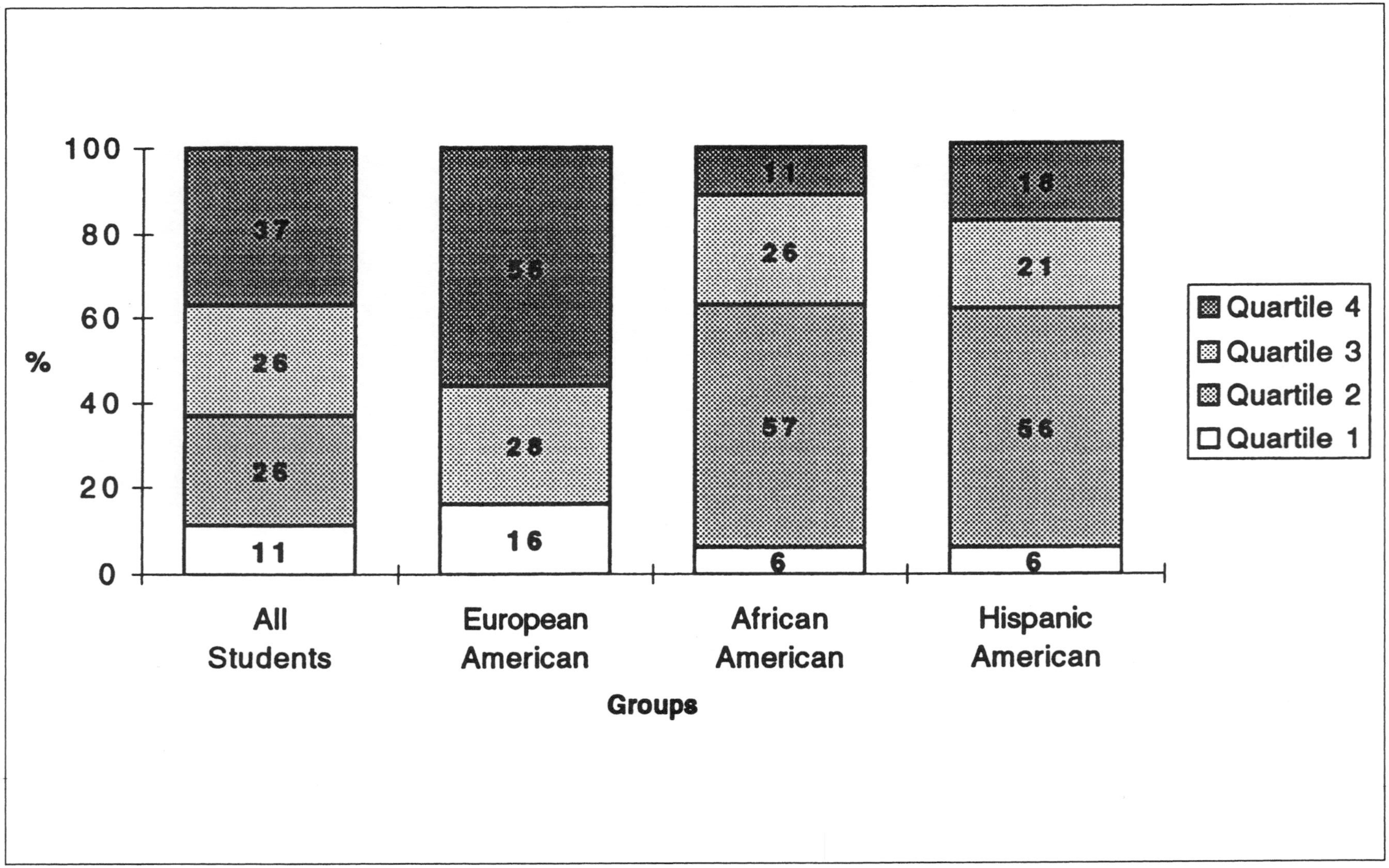

FIGURE 3.3. Run Chart of Reading Scores

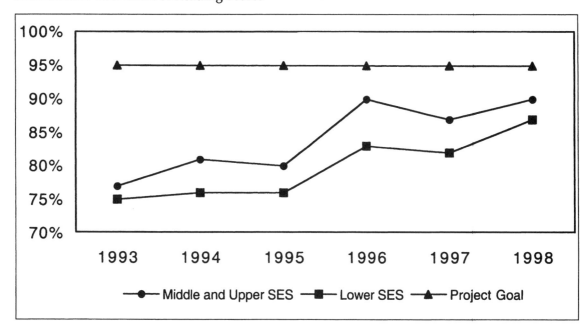

time now and use the data as a baseline. As the same data are analyzed every year, a run chart is gradually developed.

Whom to Involve. As with all work using data, those who participate in the process under study must be involved in collection and analysis.

Materials Needed. Construction of the run chart itself can be done with pencil and paper or by using computer graphics.

Tips for Facilitators

The left-hand, vertical side of the run chart is called the y-axis and usually shows the criteria or factor being analyzed, such as percentage of dropouts or number of absences. The horizontal line across the bottom of the run chart is called the x-axis and represents the time being measured, such as class periods, days, or years. Be sure to clearly label both the vertical and horizontal axes.

One problem with a run chart is that observers tend to overreact to any fluctuation in the line. They may give themselves too much credit for any upturn or become overly dismayed by any downturn. A general rule is to look for at least seven data points in a consistent direction before concluding that true change has occurred. It is interesting that this recommendation from statisticians corresponds so well with comments by educational change experts, who say that it takes 5 to 7 years to institutionalize new practices.

For Example: Closing the Gap

The school that created Figure 3.2 had disaggregated its reading scores and discovered an achievement gap related to socioeconomic status (SES). The district initiatives and the school's improvement plan focused on improvement of reading performance for all students and greater equity in achievement. Figure 3.3 reports the reading scores each year of the same cohort of students tested each spring from first through sixth grade. It shows a consistent direction of improved performance and narrowing of the gap between low-SES and middle-to-upper-SES students.

Whether creating or interpreting a run chart, the scores must be clearly labeled to identify whether these are the *school's* scores through time (e.g., every class of fourth graders) or *students'* scores through time (a cohort). Both are illustrated in *Getting Excited About Data.*

Shareholder Perceptions

The histogram and run chart were introduced to help answer the question "Where are we now?" in student achievement. A school, district, or any other organization also needs to know where it stands with its customers, clients, and community.

Surveys

Purpose. In the business environment, surveys are used to measure customer satisfaction. In much the same way, school leaders use surveys to learn what shareholders think about the school. Shareholders in an educational enterprise include *internal* groups, such as students, teachers, administrators, and support staff, and *external* groups, such as parents, taxpayers without students in the home, and businesses that employ the graduates of the system. The annotated bibliography can direct you to formal surveys that have been developed with separate forms for students, staff, and parents and may include services for compiling and analyzing responses for an additional fee. The informal survey that is locally designed to get information on a specific aspect of the school, in a timely manner, is also valuable. Consultation with an expert in survey design greatly increases the usefulness of the instrument and the data it generates.

When to Use. Formal surveys, especially those packaged with forms for various shareholder groups, are most helpful when school leaders have limited experience collecting and using data. They can provide a level of comfort, a fair degree of reliability, and an aura of objectivity that is especially needed when the idea and experience of receiving outside feedback are unfamiliar. These instruments gather a wide range of overall perceptions on factors that research has linked to school effectiveness. This type of major survey should be conducted at the beginning of a school improvement process and replicated only after sufficient intervals to measure change. Many consultants suggest an interval of 3 years. Shorter, informal surveys can be used successfully at any point in a change process to gather recommendations on a specific problem or gauge reaction to a new innovation.

Whom to Involve. For many years, schools were encouraged to survey every member of every shareholder group, and results were regarded as representative because of the widespread distribution of the survey. Unfortunately, many locally developed surveys fail to ask the right questions. Few school leaders have the statistical background to ask crucial questions about the results, such as the rate of return and whether returns came from all parts of the school's attendance area. In one city, a major program decision was made at the district level on the basis of "community input." Not until implementation of the decision encountered resistance of epic proportions did someone notice that the rate of return of the surveys was just over 1% of households and that the surveys were almost entirely from one board member's jurisdiction. The use of stratified sampling is now applied more often and is described in Tips for Facilitators.

As with every other type of data analysis, it is important that those who are part of the process being studied are involved in determining how the surveys will be administered and how the results will be analyzed and interpreted.

Materials Needed. Surveys have budget implications. The formal surveys from outside sources may be expensive. For locally developed surveys, printing costs may be a factor. Internal staff time must be provided for distribution and collection. If a survey consists primarily of multiple-choice items, bubble sheets and a scanner can shorten analysis time. If surveys are to be mailed to and/or from households, postage costs must also be considered.

Tips for Facilitators

If a school leadership group is developing its own survey, it is important to devote substantial discussion time to "exactly what is it that we want and need to know." Because shorter surveys get better return rates than do long ones, the focus of the items should be on the most essential information. Item responses should also be carefully constructed. For example, if response choices are *agree, disagree,* and *don't know,* surveyors will be amazed at the degree of "ignorance" indicated when many respondents take the easiest choice. Using a reference book on survey construction or including someone with a research background on the team is strongly recommended.

A resource person can also provide a more detailed explanation of stratified sampling. In simple language, stratified sampling means deciding who the major groups are within the total population to be surveyed. Within that group, a certain percentage are chosen at random. Survey forms may be coded by number or printed on different-colored sheets of paper. When they are returned, a tally can be kept of how many returns there are from each constituency. This will influence how the responses are interpreted and used.

For Example: All Voices Count

A school in a heterogeneous area of the city wanted to gather parents' perceptions about the school and their role in it. The team had been using information from an earlier survey that indicated a high percentage of favorable responses such as "I feel welcome at my school," "I know how to get answers to my questions," and so forth. On the basis of their data, team members were puzzled by a recent letter to the editor accusing the school of being unfriendly to minority families, and they decided to repeat their survey. This time, they consulted with a parent who was also a realtor, and they determined how various neighborhoods within their attendance area were classified. Using the address field in their student database, they identified 10% of the families in each area and color coded the response sheets. Lots of pink ones came back, and the data verified their earlier survey. But almost no green or blue forms were returned. After several discussions, one member of the group initiated the idea of having the survey introduced by someone familiar to those parents, on their own territory. In one case, the association president of a subsidized housing project agreed to call people together and explain the survey. A local minister in another area agreed to invite a school representative to meet with a parent group at the church on a weeknight. The surveys were completed and returned, and they verified the letter to the editor. These parents did not feel welcome and did not know how to approach the school. As a result of this extra effort, the tone of discussions about parents who don't care changed radically, and the school began to revise its methods of parent communication and conferencing.

Focus Groups

Many experts on survey construction will recommend at least one open-ended item to allow respondents to create their own answers. The difficulty is that few school leadership groups have the skill and time to do a thematic analysis of all these varied responses. Too often, they make for great lounge reading and speculation on who might have written which comments but provide little specific direction for planning. Focus groups can meet this need for unstructured responses in a more efficient and useful way.

Focus groups are also useful in urban settings such as Seattle with multiple language communities of newcomers to America. Interpreters can be briefed on the focus group process and the questions, and sessions can be held at community centers in each neighborhood.

Purpose. The focus group builds face-to-face communication and gets more specific information than a survey might provide. Focus groups may be held to gather perceptions regarding the school's effectiveness on a particular factor, such as parent involvement. They can also be used after a survey has been given to clarify survey responses and recommend changes that would be helpful.

When to Use. A focus group can be used when you need more specific information than a survey could provide or when a question is so complex that you have not been able to construct a survey item or design response options that seem appropriate. A focus group can also be used to help analyze and interpret data already gathered.

Whom to Involve. A focus group generally includes 10 to 12 individuals who have personal experience with the question being discussed. If the issue is parent involvement, or if the purpose is to clarify parent responses to a survey or situation, the focus group should be made up of parents. In schools with racial or economic diversity, focus groups should be formed from each population so that individuals can express their views in a comfortable setting with peers. If an issue is student behavior, there may be a focus group of staff and one of parents, but the significant involvement of students themselves should not be overlooked. Ideally, parents, teachers, and students would discuss issues together, and some schools reach this point. Most schools need time to build bridges of trust and respect before a mixed group can be as candid as a focus group should be.

Materials Needed. Inviting the right people to a focus group requires knowledge of who the opinion leaders are and skill in building rapport. Other materials needed are a comfortable setting and a tape recorder or process observer with a laptop computer.

Tips for Facilitators

When contacting persons to serve on a focus group, be clear about what will be discussed and how the group will be composed. Also let participants know that their comments will be recorded for future reference but in a way that is anonymous and confidential.

Assemble the group in a circle of comfortable chairs or around a table where the participants can face each other. The facilitator should not be seated in a place that implies leadership or authority. Refreshments and an opportunity for introductions and get-acquainted chatter are important.

If a tape recorder is being used, participants must know of its use, but it should be placed in an unobtrusive location. If a process observer is taking notes on a laptop computer, that person should sit outside the circle. The advantage of using a computer is that it saves the time and extra step of transcribing from a tape. Keyboards have become much quieter, and the noise is usually lost in the sounds of the discussion after just a few minutes.

Have a few key questions prepared but don't be tied to them. Make an opening statement about why this group was formed and what type of information the school needs. Assure the group that specific examples are needed and will be held in confidence. Let the conversation flow, and resist the temptation to fill any moment of silence with another structured question. As in teaching, "wait time" produces more analytical thinking and more accurate answers.

For Example: What's Recognition?

The leadership team had administered a formal survey, based on school effectiveness research, developed by a highly respected consultant group. Most of the responses made sense. There were no surprises except for negative parent responses regarding the format of parent-teacher conferences and "student recognition." The task force was cochaired by two members of the school improvement team and included volunteers who agreed to help analyze the survey data. They were not too concerned about the parent conference item. Teachers had talked for some time about how they needed to make different arrangements for these important communication opportunities. But they *were* quite distressed about the student recognition item, and they began to list all the ways in which students were recognized for good work, good behavior, helping others, and so forth. They wondered what more they could do and were about to propose a subcommittee to explore ways to get funding from local businesses to provide more student incentives, when one member said, "I wonder what parents thought student recognition means." After a few moments of silent confusion, a first-year teacher timidly suggested, "Maybe we should ask them." It sounded like a pretty logical next move, and the principal helped identify members of a focus group, who were invited to come and discuss the items on the parent survey and what they thought of as they read them. Through the focus group, school leaders discovered that the "student recognition" parents wanted was for the principal to know their children's names and for all teachers to get to know even the students who were not in their classes and to address them by name—or at least with more respect than "Hey, kid." The face-to-face communication of a focus group shifted the attention of staff from initiating more extrinsic reward systems to looking at the culture of the school and the interactions between staff and students.

Organizational Culture and Context

When schools address the "Where are we now?" question, they need to consider their status in terms of student performance, perceptions of school effectiveness, and the organizational climate in which any change process must take place. Histograms and run charts were described as ways to portray student data. The use of surveys and focus groups to describe shareholder perceptions was discussed. Any of these can also be adapted for analysis of the school culture and context. Think, Pair, Share is a technique that helps assess the readiness of a school to examine itself and begin to improve.

Think, Pair, Share

Purpose. Unlike basic brainstorming, which relies for its value on quick generation of numerous responses without evaluation, Think, Pair, Share is designed to provide a structured opportunity to reflect on a subject before voicing participants' thoughts. Its purpose for the individual participant is to refine and clarify personal viewpoints, prepare rationale to support them, and/or mentally rehearse how to communicate them to others. The purpose for growth of a group is to share opinions honestly and openly but with greater sensitivity than in an "off-the-cuff" or "already-flown-off-the-handle" confrontation.

When to Use. Think, Pair, Share is a helpful technique to raise awareness of concerns or needs for change during the early stages of describing "Where are we now?" As Figure 1.1 indicates, it can also be used in many contexts during an improvement process to improve communication and manage conflicts.

Whom to Involve. When Think, Pair, Share is used to look at needs for change, all parties involved in the change process should be represented. In the case of school improvement, participants might include members of the site leadership group. When Think, Pair, Share is used for conflict management, participants are those who are in conflict, or their representatives if large groups are involved.

Materials Needed. Think, Pair, Share can be used with no special materials. If common themes emerge during the activity, the facilitator may wish to record them with markers on easel paper or on overhead transparencies.

Tips for Facilitators

Give participants a prompt and a time limit of 2 to 3 minutes to think about it in silence without interaction. Respond to individual learning styles by assuring participants that they may jot down notes or doodle if they so desire as they organize their thoughts. Let them know in advance that they will be asked to share their viewpoints verbally with one other person.

After the "think time" has been provided, have participants pair up and share their viewpoints. In most cases, pairs work best if they are self-selected. There may be times, however, when the topic lends itself to structured pairing, such as the Quick-Write example regarding site-based management described in Chapter 7. When Think, Pair, Share is used to address areas of conflict, the pairs consist of a member from each side of the issue.

The sharing time may be informal or carefully structured, depending on the topic and composition of the group. In conflict management settings, it may be necessary to structure an uninterrupted time for each participant, as in the active listening exercise described in Chapter 7.

After pairs have shared, ask for voluntary comments on what they learned from each other. Exercise your own judgment about whether to record these comments for future reference. Asking "How many other pairs experienced this as well?" and "Shall we make note of it as a common response?" helps guide this decision.

For Example: Magical Metaphors

Metaphors, similes, and analogies make great prompts for Think, Pair, Share. They create strong visual images, encourage creativity, generate humor, and allow concepts to be expressed in a less threatening way than direct dialogue. Think, Pair, Share can provide a wealth of information for diagnosing organizational culture when participants are asked to complete this statement:

> If my school were a (choose your own category), it would be a (choose your own example) because ————.

During the sharing time, challenge participants to identify the positive and negative values embedded in the images. The following examples were written by school teams in the United States, Hong Kong, and St. Lucia. They imply strengths and weaknesses of the organizations that can be explored further in group discussions.

> If ———— School were an automobile, it would be American made because it has many options and is changing with the times.
>
> If ———— School were a form of entertainment, it would be the Late Night Show because we're No. 1, and we put in a lot of late hours.
>
> If ———— School were literature, it would be an epic poem because of the magnitude, but only the first 12 lines are done and the poets have a long way to go to complete it.
>
> If ———— School were a government, it would be a democracy because everyone votes on everything and now we're gridlocked.
>
> If ———— School were a vacation spot, it would be Wacky Waters because you can choose to get in shallow or deep, there are slippery slides along the way, you get burned if you're not careful, it's popular and crowded, you can go home feeling that you've had a good time, and some folks are just "all wet."
>
> If ———— School were a movie, it would be *The Wizard of Oz* because we never see the man behind the curtain and we're always guessing about what things mean.
>
> If ———— School were a group of animals, it would be horses because most are trainable but some are wild.

A Variation: Recounting History

Answering the "Where are we now?" question can sometimes be made easier by asking the related subquestion "How did we get here?" The "think prompt" is to recall significant events in the school's history, including attempted innovations. Participants identify those that were successful or positive and distinguish the factors associated with them that differ from events and changes regarded negatively. The sharing time and reporting to the large group can help diagnose the legacy of change and guide change agents in their approach. Emphasis should be placed on how a new endeavor is similar to a positive change in the past and different from efforts perceived as failures. If, for example, introduction of "the new math" was an "absolute disaster" because "parents didn't have a clue what we were talking about," it is a strong message that communication with the public will be essential to any future innovation.

Flowcharting

Think, Pair, Share provides opportunities to reflect and exchange individual perceptions of the school or district culture. Organizational diagnosis also includes a close look at governance and program factors that reveal how ready the system is to undertake change—whether its routine functions are likely to enhance or inhibit the effort. This is especially true for site-based efforts, which can be well conceived at the building level but crash against insurmountable barriers within the larger organization.

Purpose. Flowcharting is a graphic way to represent steps in a process and relationships between departments or other divisions in an organization. It can be used to illustrate how a process currently works or to design an ideal process. Sometimes groups try to diagram the current process first to see where it breaks down. Sometimes groups use flowcharting to visualize how the process should take place. On other occasions, the group may divide into two subgroups. One group may draw the current process, and the other may try to construct the ideal process to compare the two.

When to Use. Flowcharting can be used at the start of a change process to develop a visual plan of the steps that will be needed, critical decision points, and timelines. It can also be used for problem solving whenever an organization senses that its processes are inefficient or redundant.

Whom to Involve. When flowcharting is used to create a new process, representatives of all shareholders should be involved. If flowcharting is used to describe existing processes or to troubleshoot problem areas, people who work with each step of the process should be involved. Trying to flowchart a process without the people who actually participate in it can create ill will that is difficult to overcome in a spirit of constructive criticism and continuous improvement.

Materials Needed. Flowcharting can be done using a computer but most often occurs first in small groups using easel paper and markers. Stick-on notes can also be helpful as an intermediate step.

Tips for Facilitators

Have the group begin by discussing what it takes to get a process completed, a product created, or a decision approved. The task is to draw each step of the process and connect it with arrows. Simple shapes should be used, such as circles, boxes, and ovals. In some cases, groups will choose a particular shape to represent a certain department, division, or group within the organization. One rule of thumb is that a diamond shape should be used to represent decision points, where arrows could go in more than one direction on the basis of the decision that is made. If there are more than seven participants, divide the group into smaller groups to complete this activity. Do not be concerned if their flowcharts do not turn out the same. Valuable learning occurs when participants realize that even within the organization and as part of the process, they do not have a common understanding of how it works.

For Example: Taking the Initiative

A middle school had begun to work with site-based management and school improvement. Initial excitement had prompted a number of innovative ideas, but most of them had foundered before implementation because their advocates did not know how to get them approved. The school site council wanted to be sure that any individual or group had the ability to bring forth a new idea and have it receive fair consideration. Members of the council spent several meetings struggling to describe such a process in words or numbered steps. Finally, a frustrated participant exclaimed, "It still doesn't seem clear. Maybe you'd better draw me a picture!" Figure 3.4 is the flowchart that was developed in response.

A Variation: Drawing From History

As school leadership groups begin to answer the "Where are we now?" question, they sometimes find themselves wondering, "How did we get to this state?" The past may need to be revisited, discussed, and laid to rest before the present can be assessed objectively to set new directions. Flowcharting can be useful in this situation as well. The shapes used can represent major events in the history of the school, such as changes of principals, new mandates from the state, shifts in student population, or internal conflicts. The diamond shape representing decision points is used to depict turning points, especially if the event caused members of the group to go in different directions. Drawing this type of flowchart can help a group understand the influence of past events and recognize what divisions or rifts may need to be healed during the readiness stage of a change process. When one school team completed flowcharting for this purpose, it discovered that many of the conflicts still being played out among the staff could be traced back 4 years to the district's attempt at implementing a merit pay plan. Once members realized how long they had been carrying old grudges, they made a commitment to bury them and move on.

Another Twist: Picturing Reality

As I worked with a steering committee in one district's boardroom, it became clear that there was a great deal of confusion about how the quality task force fit with the strategic planning process, how the district strategic planning group

FIGURE 3.4. Flowchart for an Initiative

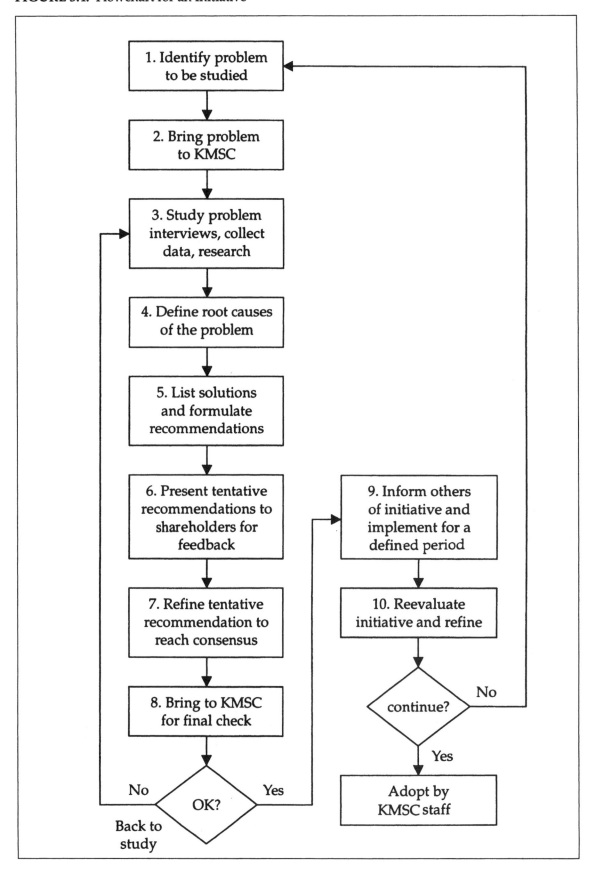

interacted with the facilities committee, how the school improvement teams fit with parent advocacy groups, and so on. The participants worked diligently to construct a flowchart and finally indicated that flowcharting was much too logical to fit the way things really happened in the district. The variation was to use any type of drawing that would illustrate how they perceived the interaction of these various groups and who they would go to for approval of building-level initiatives. Two drawings were particularly intriguing. One showed a host of colorful balloons, strings dangling, floating haphazardly across a cloudy sky, with scorch marks on several. The creators of this visual image noted that the district seemed to have a lot of lovely ideas floating around but that they did not seem connected to anything and that they never knew whether a new idea would soar or be struck by lightning.

Another group created a complex marionette, with strings attached to ears, eyes, nose, mouth, and limbs. Each of the strings was connected to a different committee or group that it had earlier tried to depict in a flowchart. The artists stated that working on a site-based team in the midst of multiple district efforts felt like being "jerked around" by the conflicting expectations of each entity, none of whom were aware of each other's work. When these two drawings were shared with the superintendent and board president, they clearly demonstrated why the schools could not move forward with site-based leadership until the district reached better consensus and integration of its own projects. Needless to say, these artists remain anonymous.

Constructing a Continuum

Flowcharting is a visual way to guide a group through discussion of how a process occurs or should occur in an organization. As a school, district, or organization analyzes its culture and context, another need often emerges. Colleagues and shareholders who begin to engage in real dialogue about an issue discover that they are not all talking about the same thing. Every group has used a common term but has unconsciously defined or interpreted it in a different way. I was in Washington, D.C., for a policy conference on site-based management when a national expert referred to the old saying "Let 'George' do it," and declared, "Site-based management is so ill defined, and the way everyone thinks it will solve everything . . . well, we might just as well call it 'George.'" Because so many districts now claim to have given their schools the freedom of site-based management, it is important to clearly define what that means.

Purpose. Constructing a continuum is a way to display the variation of perceptions and attitudes about an issue. It clarifies viewpoints by making them visual in relation to more objective factors and to the opinions of others in a group. Once it is constructed, the continuum itself can be used as a communication tool to help others understand the situation.

When to Use. A continuum can be a helpful tool for moving discussion forward when members of a group seem to talk "past" each other or slip into arguments over semantics. (Chapter 7 includes an example of the Quick-Write activity that can serve a similar purpose.)

Whom to Involve. If the issue needing definition or clarification is an internal problem of a small group, those individuals should participate in constructing the continuum. If those individuals represent larger groups, each participant could be a liaison and lead the continuum activity with his or her own group and bring back the results for further discussion in the small group. If the continuum activity has brought closure to an issue, the continuum itself can become a graphic element used by all representatives to create common explanations and messages to their constituents.

Materials Needed. All that is needed to construct a continuum is large paper and markers. An alternative is to have individuals use stick-on notes for the items or factors they perceive. This input can then be transferred and clustered on a large version for discussion in a larger group. If the group decides that the continuum that they have constructed is useful for further discussion or as part of a document for future reference, it can be re-created on software and printed for distribution.

Tips for Facilitators

Prerequisite skills for this group process activity are active listening and analytical thinking. The facilitator must be able to sense when there is a need for this type of definition and must be able to identify the opposing or mixed messages and perceptions.

The simplest continuum is a two-way arrow with the two ends labeled with terms that are in opposition. An example of this is the "Motivation Continuum" provided in *Getting Excited About Data*. Its purpose is to build commitment to the use of data in decision-making processes, while acknowledging that people accept the need to do so for a whole variety of reasons and to different degrees. The terms at the ends of the motivation continuum are *intrinsic* and *extrinsic*. More fully described in *Getting Excited About Data*, the essential outcome of the activity is to acknowledge that everyone needs to be more data oriented but that some will be motivated by a pragmatic realization that accountability is here to stay, whereas others are motivated by a deep intrinsic desire to know how to attain maximum effectiveness as an organization. Everyone's reasons are accepted and celebrated, as long as they represent acceptance of the need and willingness to participate at some level and support the overall effort.

The ability of the facilitator to identify the outcome needed is critical. In the above case, the outcome was that all participants would be able and willing to express a way in which they could support the school's work with data.

The facilitator also needs to recognize the range of ways in which that outcome could be achieved. The "Motivation Continuum" was first created when I realized that a group was struggling unsuccessfully to get all members motivated *in the same way*. Those who had a real passion for the work were angry at others for not sharing the same intrinsic drive, rather than accepting and moving forward with those who could only go as far as "I know, we're stuck with it, so just get on with it." Recognizing the range of factors and feelings within the group helps the facilitator generate the terms for the ends of the continuum. As participants generate and record their perceptions, the construction of the continuum may be revised to provide a place for all input.

Facilitator flexibility is also needed. As a group begins to place thoughts on the continuum, it may become clear that a more complex type of visual or process is needed. The facilitator needs to accept that as positive progress, not as a failure of this initial activity.

For Example: Site-Based Shared Decision Making

Figure 3.5 is an example of the need to move from a single continuum to something a little more elaborate. I was working with the school leadership teams from a large district. This district had recently developed a strategic plan and published a lovely three-color brochure assuring shareholders that all would be well with student achievement (and finance) because the district was embarking on a new approach called *site-based shared decision making* (SBSDM).

As we began to talk about the school change process and the leadership role that these groups would play, it was clear that every team had a different game plan in mind. Some thought that they would have complete autonomy to hire and fire everyone, including the principal—and this was before the first round of Chicago school reforms when a lot of principals *did* lose their jobs. Other teams actually *included* the principals, who thought the teams were going to function as advisory groups while the principals maintained their style of ultimate decision making. So there were disagreements about how the teams should operate and what issues they should address.

There was also disagreement about who should be the "sharers" in SBSDM. Some felt it was adequate to "allow" teachers to share decision making with the principal. Others had a broader reach in mind. They were thinking about the roles of support staff, parents, community members, and students—and one group even thought it would be helpful to have someone from the central office as a liaison.

Because there seemed to be two currents flowing in different directions, I created a double continuum. (If you think that this now looks like a matrix or a grid, you're right, and you can call it that, too.) The left, vertical continuum represents the stretch from most limited participation to the most inclusive mentioned in the discussion. I was able to identify the factors on this axis just by looking at people's name tags as I moved about the room. At some tables, everyone was identified with a name and the role "Teacher," while other tables had a mixture of roles represented.

The horizontal continuum represents the various definitions of an SBSDM team that were held by the groups in the room. To generate the stations along this continuum, I had to ask each group to take a piece of paper and use no more than seven words to describe themselves. This took several minutes, after which we took a break, and I constructed the first version of Figure 3.5 on a transparency.

When we returned, I showed them the continuum and asked them to interpret the meaning of the terms or labels I had used. I then asked each team to send someone to the front to put an *X* somewhere on this continuum (or grid) to represent the team's position. After lengthy discussion, and consultation with the superintendent who fortunately and commendably was present, we came to the following agreements:

◆ The far right position was not a variation that the school board was going to find acceptable or had envisioned in its strategic planning process.

◆ The far left position of principal with unilateral decision making was identified as no longer acceptable in the organizational culture being nurtured. (I knew this wouldn't fly, but here's another tip for facilitators: Sometimes it's useful to overstate the extremes at the ends of a

FIGURE 3.5. Continuum of SBSDM

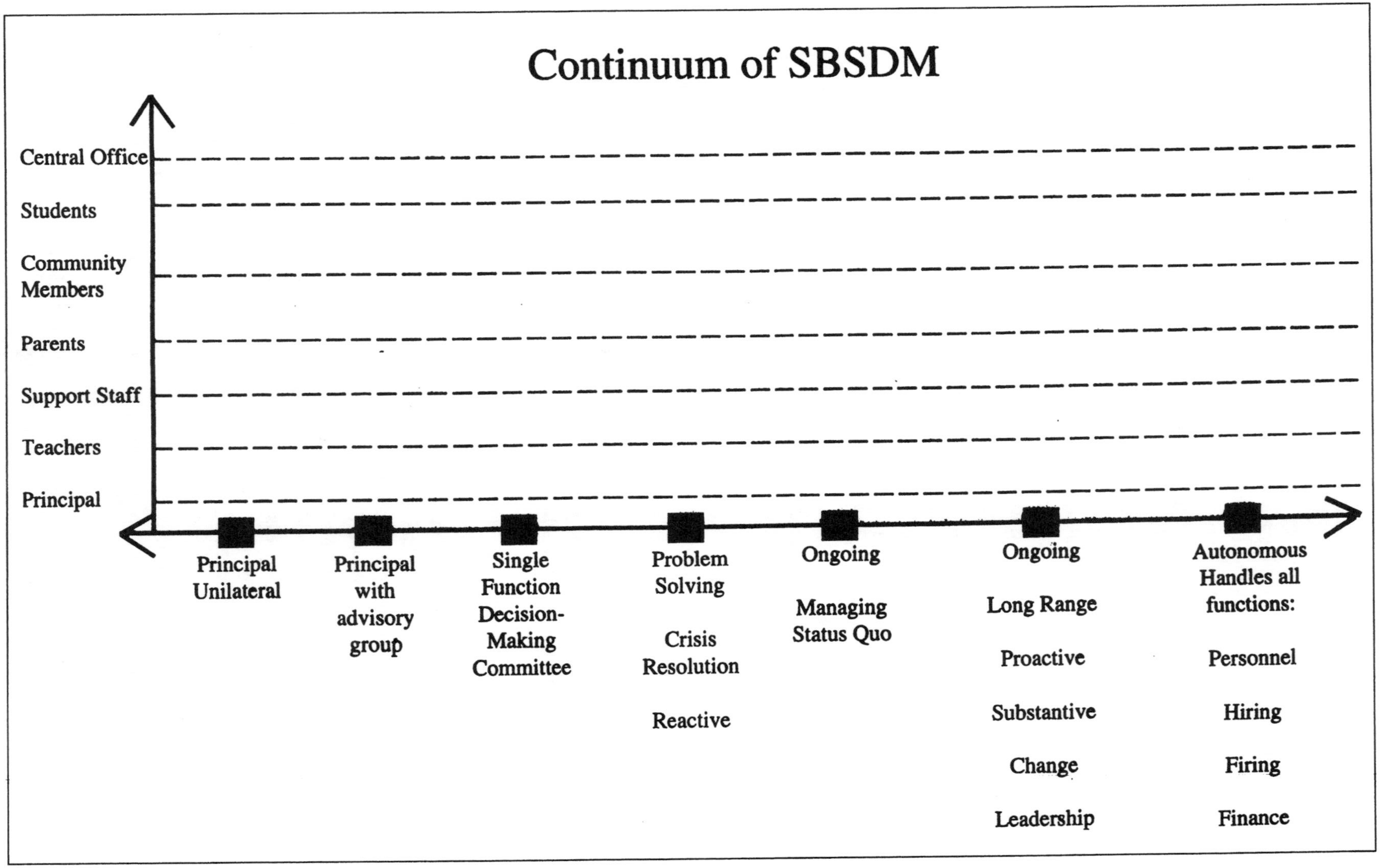

Continuum of SBSDM

Central Office
Students
Community Members
Parents
Support Staff
Teachers
Principal

Principal Unilateral

Principal with advisory group

Single Function Decision-Making Committee

Problem Solving
Crisis Resolution
Reactive

Ongoing
Managing Status Quo

Ongoing
Long Range
Proactive
Substantive
Change
Leadership

Autonomous
Handles all functions:
Personnel
Hiring
Firing
Finance

continuum. This can relieve tension by generating humor or help individual participants realize where they stand in relation to the rest of the group.)

◆ The ideal definition of an SBSDM team would be on the top line above the sixth position horizontally. This point represents an SBSDM team that includes the principal, teachers, support staff, parents, community members, students, and a central office liaison. The role of the team would be ongoing, with a long-range, proactive approach to substantive issues such as leadership for change.

◆ Not all schools would be "ready, willing, and able" to make one great leap from points on the lower left to this ideal. Each team was commissioned to take the continuum, with all the Xs on it, back to their schools. They could use it to stimulate discussion and determine "where they are now" and "where they want to go" as they move toward greater site-based shared decision making.

A Variation: CEO in Seattle

The Seattle School District has a long history of site-based management. The late Superintendent/General John Stanford described the role of principal as "CEO of your building." Some principals already operated from a naturally participatory leadership style. Others learned and applied the skills of collaboration and shared decision making. But a few took the metaphor of CEO, coming from a superintendent trained in the military, as endorsement of an authoritative approach. This variation of interpretation, coupled with a lack of definition about what should be managed at the site level and with what degree of involvement, was partially resolved through negotiated language with the Seattle Education Association.

The master agreement between the district and the association calls for collaboration on three primary functions: the school's academic achievement plan, budget, and professional development plan. Like any agreement, implementation is varied, which became a major issue in some schools. I was new to the district and had talked about site-based management during my interviews, so the director of labor relations, Mr. John Humphrie,[1] shared this challenge with me. I shared Figure 3.5 with him, and we talked about how a similar "picture" might help increase understanding of the intent and reality of the contract language.

The result of our collaboration was Figure 3.6. This graphic provides a visual explanation of several portions of contract language (notice the page number references) and places them in the context of other roles in the district, such as the board and central administration. Conflicts arising from two references to the hiring process are clarified by the high collaboration of a site subcommittee and the personnel role of the principal. This visual became a tool for training site teams and a reference for resolving individual issues and conflicts.

Rebuilding the Governance Structure: Thornton High School

Many readers will recognize the name of the Adams Twelve Five Star Schools in Colorado because the district has been a leader in school improvement

FIGURE 3.6. Site-Based Decision Making

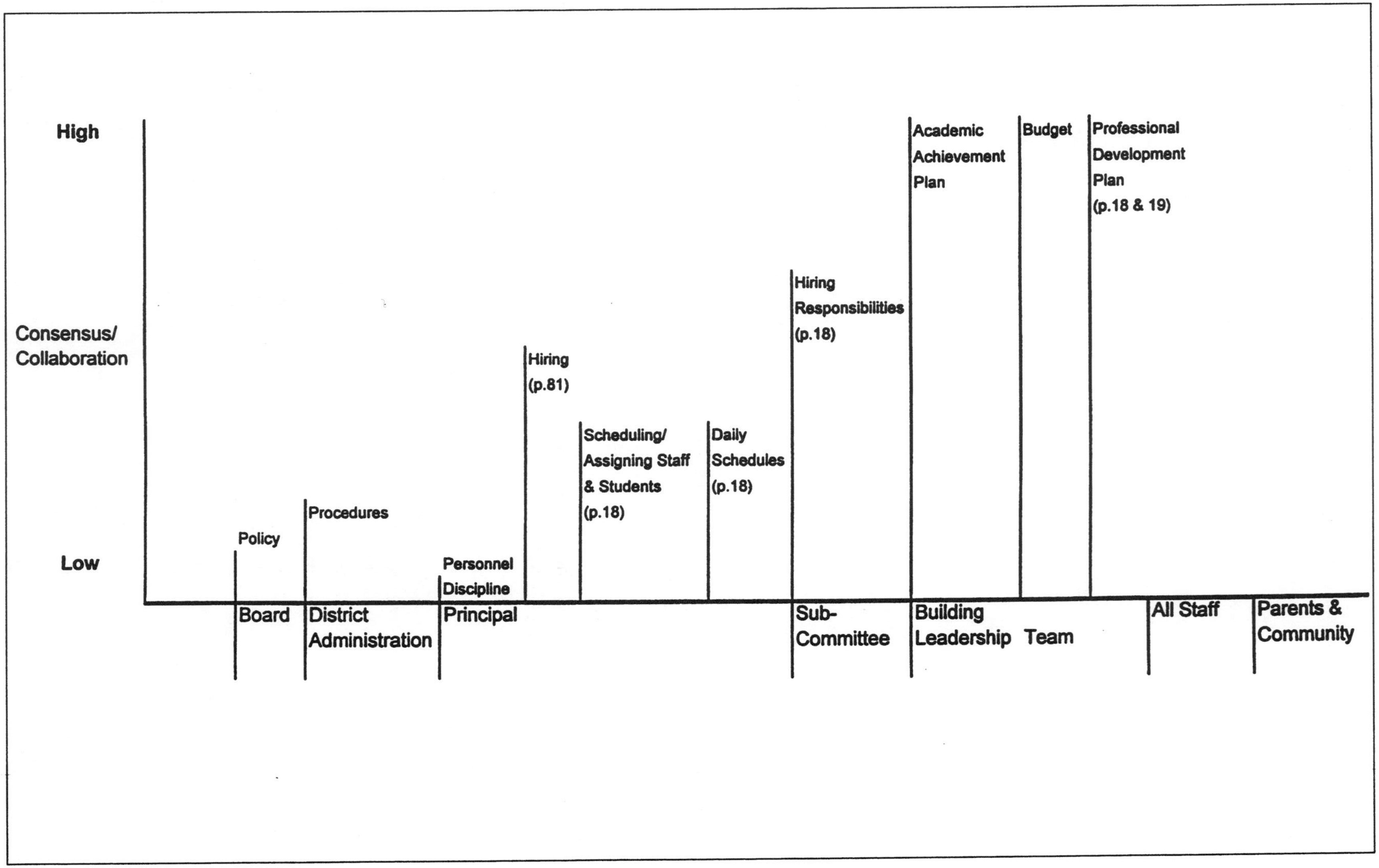

and staff development.[2] District and school staff members have shared their journey through publications and presentations, such as the "Revitalizing School Improvement" presentation at the National Staff Development Annual Conference in Dallas in December 1999. That is where I heard the story of Thornton High School.[3]

The district first began school improvement training in 1984-1985, and implementation moved at a different pace at different sites. As in most districts, it takes longest for the high schools to come on board, and it was 1994 when Thornton High School created the leadership structure shown in Figure 3.7. In addition to the leadership council, the school had an instructional leadership team, an administrative team, a school improvement team, and a full range of ad hoc and standing committees. Not surprisingly, an additional clearinghouse was needed to facilitate shared decision making between and among these various groups.

The school improvement effort continued on—faster in some schools, slower in others—but overall, the results were disappointing. The school improvement process and team were in place, but they weren't driving what happened in schools. Leaders were disappointed about a pattern of

◆ Schools not using the "tons of data" they received in decision making

◆ Malaise setting in as the excitement and energy wore down

◆ Vision statements being ignored or becoming obsolete

◆ Parents on teams not grasping the scope of school improvement as about the whole school, not their individual child

◆ Principals doing multiple plans for multiple purposes

It was time to "revitalize school improvement."

The leadership at Thornton also recognized the need to breathe new life into the collaborative work that was occurring. The first step was to review the five-year-old structure that had been created. It was cumbersome, and some still didn't understand who was doing what and why. But there were those who had a strong investment in it, so it couldn't be discarded lightly. The school improvement team and the leadership council went to work. First they analyzed the status quo of the four main existing groups and their responsibilities (see Figure 3.8). They noted the weaknesses of the existing structure but presented it as a viable option and acknowledged that sometimes "no change" is a "strength."

Although honoring the status quo, the team also went to work on alternative ways to define the roles and relationships within the school. Figures 3.9, 3.10, and 3.11 are three options that were presented to the school improvement team and leadership council. Each one was discussed and analyzed in terms of the strengths and weaknesses seen in the visual models. The leadership council voted to approve the merged format.

Figure 3.12 shows the new streamlined organizational structure, focused on goals and with a renewed sense of mission. The merged model has been effective. All the team's efforts are truly focused on the school's goals. The team regularly revisits the data that monitor progress toward the goals. Principal Kerry Moynihan says, "It's awesome."

(text continues on page 46)

FIGURE 3.7. Thornton High School Leadership Structure

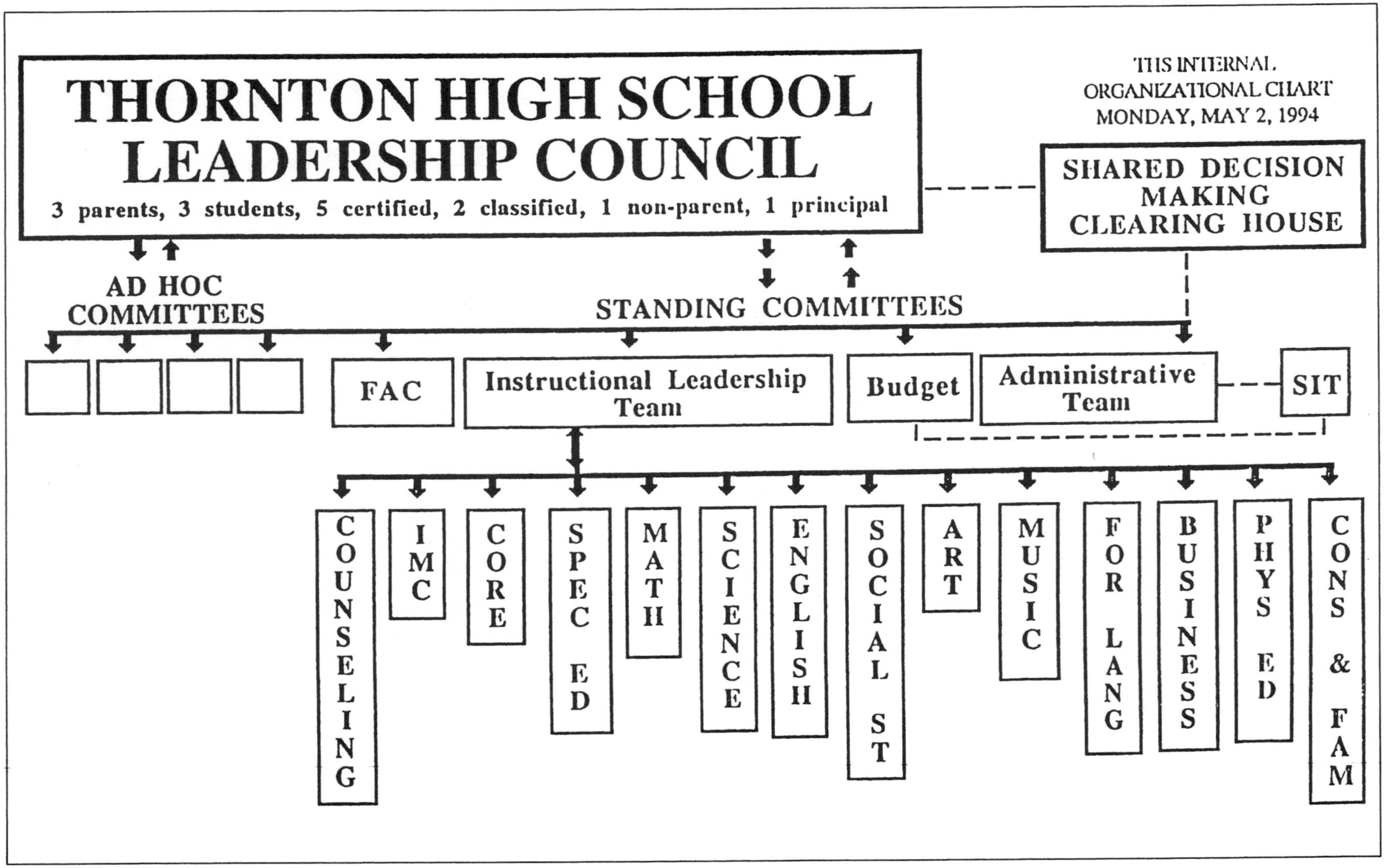

THIS INTERNAL
ORGANIZATIONAL CHART
MONDAY, MAY 2, 1994

SHARED DECISION
MAKING
CLEARING HOUSE

THORNTON HIGH SCHOOL
LEADERSHIP COUNCIL

3 parents, 3 students, 5 certified, 2 classified, 1 non-parent, 1 principal

AD HOC
COMMITTEES

STANDING COMMITTEES

FAC

Instructional Leadership Team

Budget

Administrative Team

SIT

COUNSELING

COMC

CORE

SPEC ED

MATH

SCIENCE

ENGLISH

SOCIAL ST

ART

MUSIC

FOR LANG

BUSINESS

PHYS ED

CONS & FAM

FIGURE 3.8. Restructuring Options: Status Quo

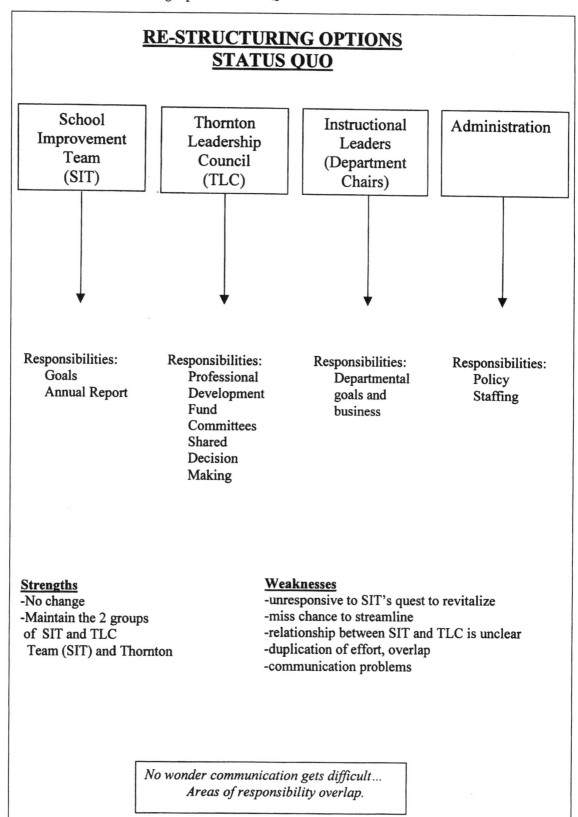

FIGURE 3.9. Restructuring Options: Option A

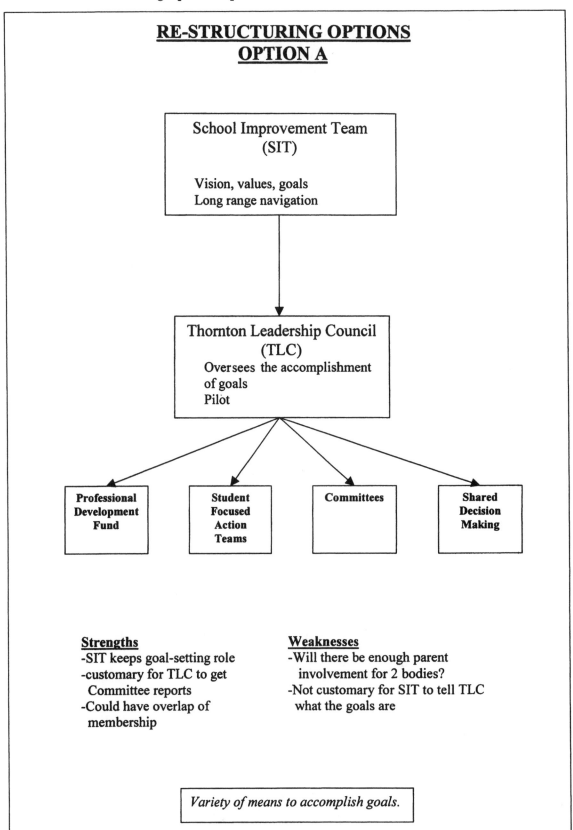

RE-STRUCTURING OPTIONS
OPTION A

School Improvement Team
(SIT)

Vision, values, goals
Long range navigation

Thornton Leadership Council
(TLC)
Oversees the accomplishment
of goals
Pilot

Professional Development Fund

Student Focused Action Teams

Committees

Shared Decision Making

Strengths
-SIT keeps goal-setting role
-customary for TLC to get
  Committee reports
-Could have overlap of
  membership

Weaknesses
-Will there be enough parent
  involvement for 2 bodies?
-Not customary for SIT to tell TLC
  what the goals are

Variety of means to accomplish goals.

FIGURE 3.10. Restructuring Options: Option B

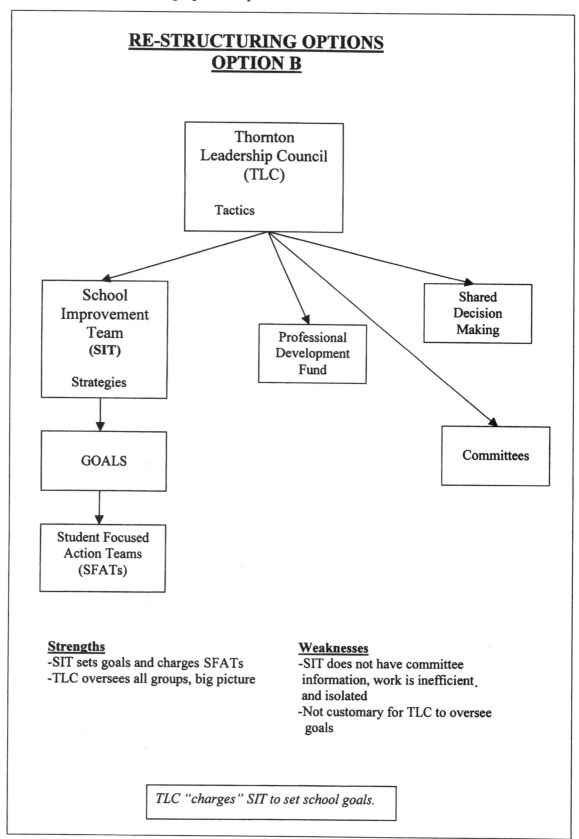

RE-STRUCTURING OPTIONS
OPTION B

Thornton
Leadership Council
(TLC)

Tactics

School
Improvement
Team
(SIT)

Strategies

Professional
Development
Fund

Shared
Decision
Making

GOALS

Committees

Student Focused
Action Teams
(SFATs)

Strengths
-SIT sets goals and charges SFATs
-TLC oversees all groups, big picture

Weaknesses
-SIT does not have committee
 information, work is inefficient
 and isolated
-Not customary for TLC to oversee
 goals

TLC "charges" SIT to set school goals.

FIGURE 3.11. Restructuring Options: Option C

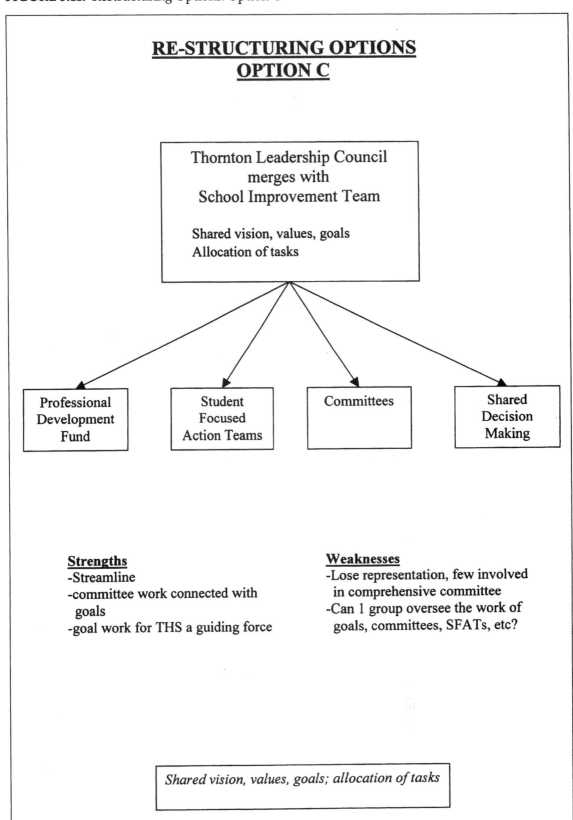

RE-STRUCTURING OPTIONS
OPTION C

Thornton Leadership Council
merges with
School Improvement Team

Shared vision, values, goals
Allocation of tasks

| Professional Development Fund | Student Focused Action Teams | Committees | Shared Decision Making |

Strengths
-Streamline
-committee work connected with goals
-goal work for THS a guiding force

Weaknesses
-Lose representation, few involved in comprehensive committee
-Can 1 group oversee the work of goals, committees, SFATs, etc?

Shared vision, values, goals; allocation of tasks

FIGURE 3.12. Thornton High School's New Organizational Structure

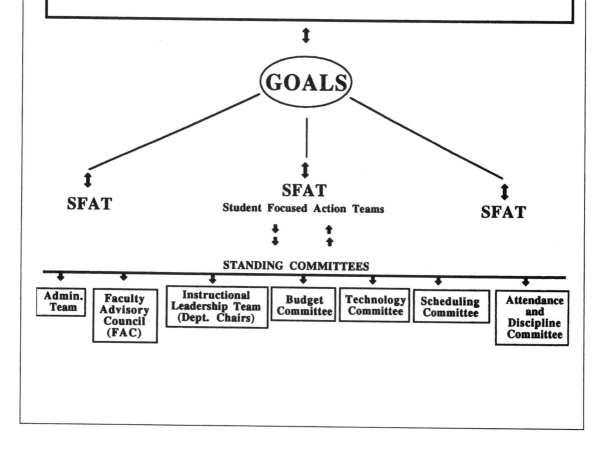

This streamlined format has now become a model for the governance structure that will be implemented in a new school. Thornton High School's determination to revisit, revise, and rededicate its efforts is also a model answer for Chapter 7's question of "How will we sustain focus and momentum?"

Notes

1. During the preparation of this second edition, my friend and colleague John Humphrie was felled by a massive heart attack after a day at the office and a basketball game in which he coached his 9-year-old son's team. Before he worked in Labor Relations, he led the district's process of ending forced busing and creating a system of school choice. John was a tall, dark, handsome African American man with a linebacker build, a passion for fly-fishing, and a heart of gold. He parked in the lot next to my office, and we would collaborate, commiserate, and make minor bets on Big Ten football through my open window. He was a soft-spoken model of listening and facilitation skills. Thank you, John, for all you did and all you were. Forgive us for not realizing the toll it was taking on you. We miss you and will honor your memory by improving and modeling the skills that made you a "bridge over troubled water."

2. In case you were too polite to ask, I wasn't. The "Twelve" comes from the way the state of Colorado numbers its school districts. The rest of the name comes from the entities that this Denver area district serves: Broomfield, Federal Heights, Northglenn, Thornton, Westminster, and parts of unincorporated Adams County. For more staff development information, contact Cindy Harrison, director of staff development (Cindy_Harrison@ceo.cudenver.edu).

3. Special thanks to Kerry Moynihan, principal, and Jan Herrera, teacher, of Thornton High School, Thornton, Colorado, for sharing the figures in this section and for follow-up and generosity. You may learn more about Thornton High School by contacting Principal Kerry Moynihan at (720) 872-4800 or Jan Herrera by e-mail (Jan_Herrera@ceo.cudenver.edu).

4

Answering the "Where Do We Want to Go?" Question

Travelers and ramblers are different, all right. Unfortunately, too many school leadership teams look like the ramblers—"all packed up and no place to go." They've assembled trunkfuls of data and worked frantically to convince their peers that things are really not so good, that they need a change, but they can't get the show on the road because they don't know where they're headed. Larry Lezotte tells school leaders that "if you don't know where you're going, any road will get you there." The problem is that it might be the wrong road, and you might end up in a spot even worse than where you are right now.

Figure 1.1 links the question "Where do we want to go?" to the planning stage in the RPTIM model and the plan stage of quality management's PDCA cycle. Leadership teams must generate broad involvement in clarifying and affirming the values of the culture. The final semantics of vision or mission and belief statements matter little compared with the powerful dialogue that can build support and commitment to a shared ideal.

The discussion and interaction that take place through the process of drafting a statement of commitment are essential. They open communication, increase interaction, and define a focus for the change process. But the rhetoric of belief statements is unavoidably general and idealistic. The written product is not the sole purpose. The process of developing it and the even more critical decisions and action taken based on it are the realities that make such activity essential. In or out of vogue, defining beliefs about why we exist is essential as an intrinsic motivator to help sustain a difficult and complex process.

Great facilitation skill is needed to move a group toward acceptance of a common belief statement. It requires exceptional creativity to transform general, idealistic rhetoric into something specific and concrete. Identifying the tangible evidence that would be seen, heard, and observed if the ideal became real is an intermediate step that must take place before strategies can be chosen to achieve it.

When school leaders think about their values in the concrete terms that would demonstrate them, the most courageous take time to compare those desired outcomes with the data that they have gathered about student performance, shareholder perceptions, and the organizational culture and context. This analysis is represented by the two-way arrow between "Mission" and "School Portfolio" in Figure 2.1. The group process tool "Monitoring Our Mission" provided in *Getting Excited About Data* assists with this compare-and-contrast activity. Discrepancies between "what we say" we do and "what we see" as our results begin the list of concerns that might be addressed through planned school change. As groups review their data, the following questions identify issues that need further examination (see Chapter 5) and suggest possible goals:

◆ What do these data seem to tell us?

◆ What do they *not* tell us? What else would we need to know—for sure?

◆ What needs for school improvement might arise from these data?

To answer the question "Where do we want to go?" also requires careful selection of priorities from among the many concerns and possibilities. Just as the well-planned traveler must make a choice from among a range of attractive destinations, school leaders must set priorities and focus their efforts where they have the greatest likelihood of creating change that lasts. Once these priorities have been established, goals can be set, study groups can identify best practices for meeting them, and progress can be monitored. Processes for building consensus, identifying observable indicators, and establishing priorities are needed to help schools and districts determine "Where do we want to go?"

Affinity Process

When I first learned about mission development, it was taught to me as an "affinity" process. Since then, I have seen the term *affinity process* used in quality management literature to describe a process similar to a force field analysis in which pluses and minuses are listed. I have not, however, found a different term to describe the process of combining ideas and topics that have a similarity, or affinity, for one another. If you find my use of the term confusing in light of your prior knowledge, feel free to change it here and on Figure 1.1 for your personal use.

Purpose. The affinity process is designed to help persons with different values find those that they hold in common. These common ideals are then put into writing and consensus is built so that they become the guiding criteria in decision making and planning.

When to Use. The most common use of this process is when a school or district is just beginning to examine itself and accept its responsibility for continuous improvement. To successfully answer the question "Where do we want to go?" an organization must identify a destination that's worth the trip. When a journey becomes difficult, it is harder to quit if the arrival is strongly desired by the travelers.

A process like this can also be helpful whenever an organization seems to be lacking focus. It should be repeated periodically to reaffirm that the same beliefs are still valued, to refine them as needed regarding changes in the environment, and to socialize new members of the organization.

Whom to Involve. "The more the merrier"—or at least the more effective. Widespread involvement from all shareholder groups is needed if the statement of commitment is to drive decision making and change. Sometimes I hear statements such as "Yes, we have a mission statement, but it doesn't mean a thing, and no one knows what it is." A few probing questions usually reveal that the mission statement was written by an individual (the new principal?) or by a small group "on retreat" and delivered as a product. Although it is the responsibility of a leader to shape a culture and reinforce positive norms, I have never forgotten this advice from Bob Garmston: "My content is not as important as their process."

Materials Needed. The most expensive resources for this process are the human resources to facilitate it and the time required to allow adequate involvement (yet the process should also move along swiftly enough to avoid getting bogged down). The number of shareholder groups and the numbers of constituents from each group who wish to participate will influence the time element. Tangible materials needed are stick-on notes, construction paper, and chart paper. A room with a large, blank wall allows the activity to take the most concrete form.

Tips for Facilitators

This process has been successfully accomplished with groups of up to 100 when the participants are divided into small subgroups for appropriate steps. First, ask participants to reflect silently about one or more prompts that are visually displayed. What is the purpose of this school? What should it accomplish for its students? What characteristics should make this school stand out from other schools? What function is uniquely ours to accomplish?

Tell them to work **independently** and write each idea on a stick-on note. Urge them to use no more than five or six words to convey a thought. Caution them not to include more than one idea on each sheet. Guide them to use positive phrases to communicate the role of the school.

The next step is to have participants form **small groups.** These may be mixed groups of school staff, parents, and other shareholders, or they may be small groups based on role. Composition of the groups is a judgment call by the facilitator, who should learn as much as possible about the history and culture of the school before accepting this responsibility. If there is great interest in participation, the initial steps of the process may be repeated at several meetings to give everyone a chance for input.

At each table, one person should introduce an idea that he or she has recorded and ask others if they have something similar. These stick-on notes should be attached to a sheet of paper. The next person around the table should introduce one of his or her ideas, ask for similar responses, and compile them on another sheet of paper. This affinity process should be repeated until participants have joined all their phrases with those of other group members.

For the next step, tell the groups to look at each sheet of stick-on notes and create a three- to five-word heading that expresses the main point or theme. Once the small groups have arrived at headings for their clusters, have them reassemble as a **whole group.** Ask one group to bring a heading sheet and post it on the wall. Repeat a similar process of asking other groups to add theirs with similar items. Continue combining sheets of notes until all work is posted.

Have participants return to **small groups** to discuss which concepts they feel are most important and what wording they see that best expresses the underlying thought. They may appreciate a sample advocacy statement ("I like this phrase because it communicates that . . .") to help them describe their preferences in a positive manner.

Charge each small group with drafting a rough statement that uses the short headings it chose to most accurately convey its members' thoughts. If these rough drafts are completed in the same setting (such as a workshop), have them shared with the **whole group.** If the steps so far have been conducted in an after-school or evening meeting, the small groups can finish their rough drafts and then submit them to the **leadership team.**

After receiving input from the groups at the workshop or from a series of meetings with shareholder groups, the leadership team begins to synthesize the main ideas from the various products and prepares a complete draft. This draft should be disseminated to **all individuals or groups** who participated in the first set of drafts. It is important to create opportunities for them to have discussion and provide direct feedback to the team, not just return the draft with written comments.

The **leadership team** uses the feedback to further revise the statement or document, but completion of the written product is not the end of the team's work. The mission or set of belief statements will guide the organization only if it is consciously and overtly introduced as a central focus for all future decision making. The team should plan a visible celebration and commitment event. Some schools have held signing ceremonies complete with special pens to commemorate the occasion. **All groups** who contributed to the process should participate in this public event. When the celebration is over, the **leadership team** has a continuing responsibility to plan ways of infusing the mission into all decision-making processes and into the culture of the school. The team may identify a subgroup or a small, separate committee and charge it to be "keeper of the vision."

Creating the statement of commitment is just the first small step in identifying what the school wants to create, the destination it seeks in response to "Where do we want to go?" Referencing and reaffirming the mission of the school throughout the change process will move it "off the wall" and "into the walk" of daily routines and practices. School leaders must challenge the organization on a regular basis with application questions such as "What are we doing to support our mission? Which of our current programs and practices are consistent with the values we espouse? Which aren't? Are the things we measure and assess the things that we say are truly important?" One of the school leadership team's responsibilities is to plan activities that will consciously and intentionally inculcate the school's values into its cultural norms. Some ways to continually affirm the values of the organization are discussed in Chapter 7.

For Example: Mission Statements

The following mission statements were developed through the process described above. They are clear and concise, are strongly worded, and convey a sense of the organization's responsibility to accomplish them.

The staff of ——— School believes that *all* students can learn and can achieve mastery of basic grade-level skills, regardless of their previous academic performance, family background, socioeconomic status, race, or gender. We believe that our school's purpose is to educate all students to high levels of academic performance while fostering positive growth in social and emotional behaviors and attitudes. We accept the responsibility to teach all students so that they can attain their maximum educational potential.

The mission of ——— is to help students acquire the knowledge, skills, and attitudes necessary to become healthy, happy, productive adults; to help students become enthusiastic lifelong learners who are able to manage change; and to help students perpetuate and improve the democratic process and have an impact on their communities, their country, and the world.

——— Schools will create an accountable learning community that encourages all students to achieve, to their highest potential, the knowledge and skills needed to be fulfilled, productive members of a changing society.

An Accordion Note

In the group process described earlier, bold print was used to identify the roles of individuals, small groups, the whole group, and the leadership team. The expansion and contraction from individual work to small groups to large groups and back to small groups may be visualized with the metaphor of playing an accordion. The leadership team orchestrates the movements of the accordion. The more support it will need to accomplish a task, the more it will need to expand the accordion and bring in a greater volume of air and energy.

Brainstorming

Too often the intense involvement of developing a commitment statement or set of beliefs has no impact because it does not direct the action of the organization. It's like a rambler saying, "I'd sure love to take the perfect vacation" without determining what criteria would make a vacation "perfect." Travelers, on the other hand, are more likely to say, "The perfect vacation spot would be quiet, isolated, with lots of sunshine, moderate temperatures, and hiking trails."

Purpose. Brainstorming generates as many ideas as possible related to a particular problem, issue, or goal. It is not tied to current reality, as are the processes described in Chapter 3. Brainstorming is designed to add new ideas to the status quo.

When to Use. You can tell from the number of Xs in the brainstorming column on Figure 1.1 that this is a versatile group process. It can be used for many reasons at almost any point in a change process. It is described here as a follow-up phase after affirming the values of an organization. The specific purpose and timing are to make the mission more concrete by identifying observable indicators that would prove the mission was being accomplished.

Whom to Involve. Active participation by a broad range of constituents from all shareholder groups was recommended for affirming the value system of the organization. Smaller groups with an understanding of the educational enterprise will be better able to contribute to this phase.

Materials Needed. Brainstorming requires open minds, markers, and poster paper.

Tips for Facilitators

Although brainstorming is versatile, it is not as simple as it looks. Facilitators must not assume that groups know how to use it effectively. Begin by reviewing the rules of brainstorming with participants:

- ◆ Quantity is more important than quality.
- ◆ Share every thought that occurs to you.
- ◆ Make no evaluative statements.
- ◆ Listen carefully to group members.

Focus the brainstorming on the problem or purpose. When addressing the "Where do we want to go?" question, the need is to focus on the tangible evidence that we could see and hear if an organization were living by its beliefs. A helpful phrase to use with groups is "observable indicators." This phrase acknowledges that some important aspects of school life are not measurable in the traditional sense of a quantified assessment but should be observed in the behavior of its members.

Record every idea that is expressed, in the words of the speaker. Do not edit or combine with others that you think are the same. Set a time limit of 10 to 15 minutes to create a sense of urgency. Within that time, be comfortable with moments of silence. The next contributions are usually even more creative and perceptive than those before a lull in the action.

For Example: Lifelong Learner

The mission statement was brand new. It included phrases about basic skills, responsible citizenship, and respect. The school leadership team felt quite confident about writing goals and action plans consistent with those ideals. But the members were stumped by the phrase "lifelong learner." How would they incorporate that into their improvement plans and verify whether they accomplished it? One member sardonically remarked, "Yeah, right! Now our postgraduation follow-up studies have to track them down at age 70!"

The prebrainstorming challenge was for group members to first think individually of someone they considered to be a lifelong learner. The brainstorming task was to list what they had seen that person do, or heard that person say, that convinced them that she or he was a lifelong learner. The list included items such as "gets interested in something," "goes to the library to find out more about it," "is open to doing new things," "starts projects on her own," "tries to get other people interested," "keeps after it until he knows all there is to know and then is on to something else," and "likes to figure out her own way to do it." It was a fascinating list, but the group wondered how helpful it would be because they were describing adults.

The next challenge was a variation on the same theme. On the basis of the age of the students they parented or taught, smaller groups were formed and challenged to brainstorm "What does each of those behaviors look like at age 17? at age 11? at age 7?" This second round of brainstorming yielded two results. One was the conclusion that most of those behaviors looked pretty much the same at any age and could be observed in the school setting. The other was a realization that many of the school's practices in grouping and scheduling limited a student's ability to demonstrate those behaviors.

Brainstorming is useful in the "Where do we want to go?" stage to set some criteria that distinguish the desired state from the status quo. These criteria also become factors to assess as the group monitors its progress.

Nominal Group Process

A mission statement helps describe where the organization wants to go, and brainstorming observable indicators generates criteria to make the statement more tangible. A third important part of answering this question is setting priorities for improvement.

Purpose. Despite general agreement about what the school should accomplish for its students, there is still a wide range of viewpoints about which aspects of the school should be improved to do so more effectively. Nominal group process gives everyone an opportunity to participate in selecting which areas to work on first.

When to Use. Because it is never possible to address everyone's concerns about the school, nominal group process is used in the planning stage to select priorities. It can also be used to reach consensus on other important decisions throughout a change process. The nominal group technique is particularly helpful in situations in which powerful individuals have a habit of dominating discussions and where "competing for airtime" has been the prevailing way of gaining influence.

Whom to Involve. All interested parties should be invited to participate. They must be made aware that nominal group technique will be used and that it is a structured process designed (and tested and proved effective) to allow an equal voice for all participants.

Materials Needed. The sequence of steps and rules for nominal group process should be posted. The facilitator will need markers, poster paper, an easel, and tape. Index cards or stick-on notes will help participants with their ranking.

Tips for Facilitators

Post and provide an overview of these steps before beginning:

◆ Individual brainstorming

◆ Round-robin listing

◆ Individual ranking of priorities

◆ Tabulation of ranks

◆ Discussion

◆ Individual ranking

◆ Tabulation of ranks

Call attention to the fact that by design, "discussion" is far down the list. The sequence was developed to provide an opportunity for all ideas to be generated and included through brainstorming and to encourage individual reflection and decision making before group members begin to influence each other.

Stimulate the **individual brainstorming** step by posing a question such as "What are all the things that anyone might say could be improved about our school?" As the question is displayed, underline the word *all* and emphasize that this is their opportunity to create a comprehensive list for consideration and that they should be candid and list every concern they have. Call attention to the word *anyone* and remind them to present not only their viewpoints but also others of which they are aware. This is an opportune time to review results of survey data and be sure that the concerns of constituents are included, even if they are not present to participate. Stress that the word *could* expresses our commitment to continuous improvement and does not imply that the current situation is abysmal. Groups are often reassured and encouraged to be open by the statement that "when we talk about improvement, we're not thinking 'horrible-to-wonderful.' We're thinking 'good-better-best.'"

Observe the individual brainstorming and allow plenty of time until most participants seem to be done writing. Emphasize that every one of their concerns will be included but that it will be helpful if they look them over to be sure that they are specific and easily understood. Suggest that longer statements be reduced to a short three- to five-word phrase. Mention that a concern such as "student test scores" will be more helpful if it is broken down into more specifics such as "reading achievement" or "math problem solving." Even if that makes their list longer, it is good to subdivide such general items because reading scores and math scores would be approached differently if they became the school's goals.

If the group consists of 15 or fewer participants, serve as recorder and conduct the **round-robin listing** step of the process. If you are working with a large group, divide it into smaller units and have members select recorders. The recorders can give their lists to another participant who will be sure that items from both lists are included.

Round-robin listing means that each person states one concern from his or her list, and this is repeated around the circle. Emphasize that everyone must listen carefully and cross off the list concerns that other persons mention to avoid duplication and keep the process moving quickly. The recorder should assign a letter to each item (see "For Example" below) to facilitate ranking and discussion later.

If you have facilitated a small group, you now have one list of all concerns. If you divided a large group into smaller groups that represented different schools, each group has its own total list and will rank those items. If everyone in a large group was from the same school, however, you need to take a break and combine the separate group lists into a total master list. This can be done quickly during a break for the large group, either by repeating the round-robin exercise or by word processing all the responses and then printing the master list for each participant.

When the list of "all the things that could be improved" has been completed, give each person five index cards or slips of paper. Direct participants to choose the five items they are most concerned about and to put the letter of each one on a separate slip. If a group member is most concerned about the items labeled *A, E, J, M,* and *P,* there would now be a card or slip of paper with a letter *A*, another with *E*, a third with *J*, and so forth. Then tell the group it must further prioritize the items by shuffling them around until the most important concern is at the top, and the other four are lying on the table or held in the hand in descending order. The group should then put a number 5 on the top one, a 4 on the next, and so on down to 1. These directions must be clear, and you should check to see that they are being followed correctly. If you do not check them, some participants will **rank** their concerns in reverse order from the rest of the group. A value of five should represent their top priority, so that the highest total represents the greatest concern when all are compiled.

After ranking their items, members should rearrange their cards in alphabetical order. The recorder may call out a letter, and each person who ranked it states the numerical value he or she gave it. The recorder should write down each ranking, rather than just add them mentally and record a total. When discussion takes place, it will make a difference whether one concern has a total value of 20 because 10 persons ranked it a 2 or because 4 persons ranked it a 5.

Discussion begins after the rankings have been tabulated. By this time, almost every group can see agreement beginning to emerge around top-priority concerns. In some cases, a second round of **ranking** and **tabulating** is unnecessary because the priorities become clear and the discussion does not indicate any strong disagreement with them. If there is disagreement or if questions are raised about some items, ask those who "gave it a 5" to share their reasons for being so concerned about it. Sometimes their responses will provide new information for other participants and cause them to shift their priorities. On other occasions, questions will raise the need for more accurate information before a final decision is reached. In this situation, help the group decide what information is needed, who can provide it, and how much time will be needed to get the information. Then schedule another meeting to look at the information before a second round of ranking determines the school's priorities.

For Example: The Top Three

The charts generated by one team at a workshop looked like this:

A.	Classroom management	5, 5, 1, 3, 5, 4	23
B.	Teacher punctuality	—	—
C.	Parental involvement	2, 5	7
D.	Time on task	5, 4, 2	11
E.	Teacher motivation	3	3
F.	Community participation	—	—
G.	Student evaluation	4, 3, 5, 5, 1	18
H.	Physical environment	—	—
I.	Quality of instruction	2, 4, 4, 5, 4, 5	24
J.	Teacher evaluation	4, 3	7
K.	Discipline	—	—
L.	Student involvement	—	—
M.	Pupil-teacher rapport	3	3
N.	Interpersonal relationships	2	2
O.	Staff development	3, 3, 2, 3, 2	13
P.	Cocurricular activities	1	1
Q.	Principal-teacher relations	—	—
R.	Teacher involvement in curriculum development	—	—
S.	Instructional leadership	5, 4, 5	14
T.	Staff supervision	2, 2, 1, 1	6
U.	Communication	—	—
V.	School's curriculum	—	—
W.	Student motivation	—	—
X.	Staffing configuration	—	—
Y.	Empowerment	—	—
Z.	Homework policy	—	—
AA.	Instructional materials	—	—
BB.	Grantwriting	—	—

Completion of the nominal group process focused the school on the quality of instruction, classroom management, and student evaluation. Goals were written for each of these concerns. Although the interest in staff development did not surface as one of the top three priorities, its presence in the list encouraged the district to offer workshops related to the three goal areas that emerged.

A Variation: Goals Before and After Data

The nominal group process is a good way to give all participants an equal voice in setting priorities. There is a weakness inherent in starting with brainstorming, however. Too often, members of the group contribute concerns that arise only from their personal awareness. Sometimes the priorities that emerge have little connection with the beliefs that the school or district has created as its ideals. Of even greater concern is the omission of concerns that were revealed by the data analysis done in response to the "Where are we now?" question.

A variation is to schedule a review of the statement of commitment and a short summary of the findings of the data shortly before the meeting at which the nominal group process will be conducted. Those who attend this review should be encouraged to think about the findings and participate in setting priorities for improvement. On a smaller scale, the facilitator may remind the group to think briefly about the organization's values and the data summaries that have been available for study and urge group members to include that information as they list areas of concern.

The influence of data on the priorities and direction of school improvement plans became obvious to me in a large district that I visited several times. On each trip, I provided school improvement training to a different group of school teams. Data from statewide assessments became available midway through this multiphase training effort.

Priority concerns identified by nine schools *before* state test data were received are listed below. (The list totals more than nine because each school chose from two to five goals.)

Student attendance	3
Teacher attendance	3
Reading achievement	2
Student discipline	2
Home-school communication	2
Parent involvement	2
Math achievement	1
Quality of teaching	1
Minority achievement gap	1
Meaningful staff development	1
Student motivation	1
Parent commitment	1
Teacher commitment	1
Internal school communication	1

Priority concerns identified by nine similar schools *after* state test data were received by the district are as follows:

Reading achievement	8
Math achievement	5
Attendance	3
Student discipline	2
Parent involvement	1
Curriculum planning	1
Conflict resolution	1
Time to "do all this"	1
Home-school relations	1

Team functioning	1
Closing minority gap	1
Writing achievement	1
Staff buy-in	1
Student self-esteem	1

Eight of the nine teams who had test data before them and had reviewed the data prior to goal setting focused their priorities on student achievement, compared with two of nine that had not considered test data before the goal-setting activities.

Another Twist:
Adding Mission and Reality

The previous example demonstrated how a review of the school's **data** helped focus the goal-setting process. Two other elements have turned out to be useful as shareholders deal with the critical step that will determine their route and destination as they continue the journey of school change. One of these elements is the **mission** of the organization. Priority should be placed on concerns that have a tight alignment and direct impact on whether the school really lives by its stated values. The other element is the hard reality that some factors that desperately need attention may lie outside the immediate sphere of influence of the school. Energy should be invested in goals that are within the **power of the school** and are amenable to change.

Getting Excited About Data includes a combination of the nominal group process from this chapter and a decision matrix, described in Chapter 5. That tool "forces" reflection by asking participants to rate each area of concern in three columns. The first column asks **"How severe?"** the situation is and directs participants to consider the data and rate each item from 1 to 5, with a 5 representing a concern that has actual data to demonstrate that it is a severe problem. The second column asks **"How crucial?"** and refers to the school's mission statement. Concerns are rated a 5 if they are absolutely essential and critical to the school's ability to live up to its promises. The third column asks **"How responsive?"** and acknowledges that some concerns are more amenable to change and within the power of a school than others. (My initial fear that this column would provide an escape route from the complex issues was unfounded. I have discovered a strange paradox. Allowing participants to voice the fear that "we can't do anything about that" seems to pique the creativity and/or stubbornness of others, who begin to think of ways they might.)

An item rated 5 is one that members of the school community have a sense of efficacy about tackling. Using this decision matrix, the "ideal" goal would be rated a 15. It's a severe situation that is critical to the school's mission and that the school itself can change.

Color Coding

Color coding is not so much a group process as a way of identifying the sources of responses. In Chapter 3, printing surveys on different-colored sheets of paper was described as a way to be sure that results include representation from all groups or neighborhoods. If separate meetings are held for various shareholders to participate in the mission development process, different colors of stick-on notes can be used at each session. As responses are grouped, a visual scan can help ensure that contributions from all groups are included in the final product. Color coding can also be used when activities such as the nominal group process are conducted to establish priorities.

Purpose. Color coding shows which concerns or priorities are of most interest to which participants. This information may help school leaders find interested persons to help with change efforts. It can also highlight concerns that may need informal attention, although they do not emerge as the shared priorities of the overall group.

When to Use. Color coding may be used when there is more than one set of priorities or when more than one set of volunteers is needed to carry out a series of tasks.

Whom to Involve. It is repetitious, but important, to note again that all who may be affected by a change or expected to help assist with its implementation should be included in determining the priorities.

Materials Needed. The facilitators will need chart paper, markers, and tape. Each participant will need a predetermined number of colored stickers or stars. The number of colors needed will depend on the range of constituent groups participating in the process.

Tips for Facilitators

Use brainstorming to generate the list of concerns or problems that participants feel should be addressed. This step is the same as the beginning of the nominal group technique, but the rest of the process is less formal. After the list of items has been recorded on large chart paper, be sure that each participant has five dots or stars of the appropriate color. Have participants go to the charts and place their five dots or stars by the five items that they consider to be top priorities for most immediate attention.

For Example:
Curriculum Priorities

The district had been without a curriculum director for several months. Even before that, work on instructional programs and assessment had virtually ground to a halt because of budget cuts. An interim administrator was assigned to determine the areas that most needed attention and to set up a timeline for addressing them as funds became available. Because the district no longer had curriculum specialists, these assignments had been divided among the principals in addition to their building-level responsibilities. A method was needed for setting priorities and organizing work on them in the most efficient manner.

The first step was to brainstorm the list of issues and projects that had been neglected and needed attention. Once the list was complete, central office administrators were given five gold dots, secondary principals were given five purple dots, and elementary principals were given five green dots. A quick visual scan of their responses identified two issues that had multicolored responses and would be handled in a K-12 setting. Other issues that had only purple or green dots could be set aside to be addressed in subcommittees that were just secondary or elementary in composition. A few issues remained on the list for attention at some future date, but the delay would not cause any hurt feelings because the items had no preponderance of dots of any color.

Weighted Voting

Color coding helps show differences in the responses contributed by different individuals or groups. Through weighted voting, participants can show the relative value that they place on different issues. They can show that they feel more strongly about some concerns than about others.

Purpose. Weighted voting provides a measure of the relative importance placed on various items by individuals and groups.

When to Use. Weighted voting can be used when "not all items are created equal" in the eyes of the participants. If a participant in the color-coding activity had said, "Can I put all my five dots on just one thing?" it would have been a signal that weighted voting could be used.

Whom to Involve. The same persons who would have been part of the other priority-setting activities would also be involved in weighted voting. This process is particularly appropriate when the participants will bear primary responsibility for the tasks that are identified. It gives them a greater opportunity to determine where they will invest their energies.

Materials Needed. The facilitator will need chart paper, markers, and tape. Each participant will need a predetermined number of dots, stickers, or labels, but they may all be the same color.

Tips for Facilitators

Start by having participants brainstorm the issues to be addressed or the tasks to be done, in the same way that the nominal group process began. As in color coding, the participants have five dots or stickers. The uniqueness of weighted voting is that participants may distribute their five dots (or votes) in any combination. If they feel that one item is crucial for immediate attention, they can use all five of their dots to indicate its importance. If they want to be sure that attention is given to two items, they may use two dots for one and three for the other. Depending on the number of participants and the length of the brainstormed list, the facilitator may allocate more or fewer than five votes per participant.

For Example:
Making the Workshop Work

They had been teaching all day, it was hot, and the room had no windows. Because of budget cuts, the schools were not allowed to hire subs for professional development activities, so we were going to meet from 4:00 to 7:00 on three consecutive evenings. It was precious time, and the people donating it to learn how to function as a school leadership team were precious, too. Meeting their needs and making the content relevant were essential—but it was clear that they came with a range of expectations so varied that it could not possibly be addressed in 9 hours of less-than-prime learning time. The challenge was to focus the agenda in some way that would clearly show respect for their time and priorities. Knowing that we could not include them all, we listed the topics they had anticipated and gave five stars to each participant. As they left the first evening session, they placed their stars on the list to express their priorities. The results looked like this:

Selecting strategies related
to curriculum   *****************

Process used to develop
implementation plan   *********************************

Timelines   *********

Moving from departmentalized to
multidisciplinary   ********

Team skills   ********************************

Strengthening our belief system   ************

How to use data in decision
making   *******************

Ways to gather data   ******************************

Motivating students with no role   ***
models or hope   **

Difference between making
easy and hard changes   **********

How to avoid bandwagons   ******************

Difference between school
improvement and strategic
planning   ***

It was clear that the strongest interest of the participants related to student motivation, which was no part of the planned training. Fortunately, the next set of priorities (development of action plans combined with timelines, teamwork skills, and gathering and using data) was part of the planned agenda. I was able to focus on those topics while having my materials on student motivation Express Mailed to me for the last session. Participation in the weighted voting activity created a high level of commitment that overcame the poor timing and conditions. Because they could see the needs expressed by the whole group, those whose topics were omitted understood and accepted that result.

One comment on the evaluation sheet read, "This is the first time I've felt like I had some control over what we did in a workshop. I didn't mind the evenings, because I was getting what I came for." One way to turn ramblers into travelers is by using group process techniques to help them shape their own destination as you address the question "Where do we want to go?"

5

Answering the "How Will We Get There?" Question

Heard the one about how to spot the "big wheels" in an organization? They're the ones who are always going in circles.

Too many school change efforts go nowhere because the leaders confuse choosing the destination or goal with having a plan. Although change processes must be flexible enough and adjusted often enough to be considered evolutionary, the initial implementation plan must be specific enough to let everyone know what's expected.

Development of a plan or map for the journey blends planning, training, and implementation aspects of the RPTIM model, shown in Figure 1.1. Training is needed in *how* to plan, and the plan itself will identify needs for *more* training about best practices and how to implement appropriate strategies. In the Three *Is* model, this phase includes implementation of the school change process itself, within which specific strategies are identified and initiated. In the PDCA cycle of quality management, answering the "How will we get there?" question is the planning stage.

Addressing the "How will we get there?" question requires organizations to be honest about why they are not there yet. The "Study" box before "Strategies" on Figure 2.1 emphasizes the need for thoughtful analysis and new learning before leaping straight into action. The three points in the "Study" stage represent three types of inquiry:

◆ Study of relevant research

◆ Study of best practice in other schools and districts

◆ Further study of the school's practices and local factors related to the goal

The tools in this chapter include the cause-and-effect diagram and force field analysis for exploration of these local factors. Advance organizers are introduced that help a school analyze its programs, and a flowchart guides discussion of school and district roles in improving student achievement.

For any problem, there are multiple solutions, and organizations such as schools that have limited resources and high visibility need to choose those most likely to produce the intended results. Use of a decision matrix improves choices of strategies. Development of the action plan for each new strategy is relatively simple in concept but requires discipline and perseverance to work out the specific steps needed, decide who will be involved and who will take primary responsibility, align the resources that will be needed, and project a timeline that keeps things within the scope of "humanly possible."

In the classroom, we know that we must make thorough lesson plans yet be willing to surrender them to the teachable moment. In the same way, we must make careful and complete plans for school change, pursue them with power and passion, yet hold them lightly enough so we can monitor and adjust as we go.

Study Relevant Research

Chapter 4 emphasized the importance of shareholder involvement that builds commitment around goals that are supported by data and closely reflect the core values of the organization. How demoralizing it is then when strategies are selected by brainstorming on the basis of existing knowledge, are implemented without learning from other sites, and end up failing to produce the intended results.

Once the goals have been established, study groups (also called subcommittees, task forces, etc.) should be formed to investigate the situation thoroughly and bring forward recommendations for the strategies or interventions to be implemented. Three important areas of study are research, best practice, and deeper analysis of the current situation.

Others may have a different set of definitions, but I distinguish research from best practice in this way. *Research* is the body of literature that represents current theory and findings from studies conducted by people who are full-time scholars, not practitioners. For example, neurolinguistic science and brain research include theory and investigations that we should be following closely. New discoveries about language acquisition are important if we're concerned about development of reading skills or the arrival of students learning English as a second language.

If we have goals related to students' behavior and social development or character development, we should become knowledgeable about the literature on resiliency and the studies about youth assets. But in this particular context, what I classify as research provides only information. It may define the "what" and may suggest some "should's." But this type of research doesn't—and wasn't designed to—answer the educators' all-important question of "how." To move from information to application, we have to connect with those who have begun to put the research into practice.

Explore Best Practices

Exploring best practice sounds simple—but it comes with a price tag. It means that teachers reach out to other teachers, schools reach out to other schools, and districts reach out to other districts. It requires us to admit to other people that we don't have all the answers and that—although we're doing a good job—we want to do even better than we are presently.

School leaders and shareholders will have more and more creative ideas, but here are three basic avenues to explore to learn about best practices: literature, site visits, and Web sites. Literature about implementation includes practical research such as the reports conducted on Chicago school reform. Journal articles that report on "lessons learned from . . . " fall into this category. In his new book, *Accountability in Action,* Doug Reeves describes "90/90/90 schools." These are schools that serve a student population with 90% or more of the students from minority groups, 90% or more considered economically disadvantaged, *and* 90% or more reading above standard. The leadership team of any school with the first two factors should pursue these schools to see how they accomplished the third.

Visits to other schools and districts have a powerful impact on both the visitors and the visited. Word of mouth and consultation with staff members in the state department of education and regional agencies will help identify potential partners. Be specific when you ask around about schools or districts that model "best practices." Mention the goal you are trying to achieve, the barriers you perceive, and the characteristics of a school or district you want to visit.

Test out the recommendations you're given by verifying whether these sites are getting the type of results you want from their innovative practices. Take into consideration their location and characteristics. For example, in Washington State, a principal can query the state database to find schools with similar demographics that had superior performance on the state assessment. These would be schools to contact or visit.

Don't make the proverbial "no one's a prophet in his or her own country" mistake. In other words, don't overlook the possibility that there may be best practice examples right within your district or just down the road. Under the leadership of Director Aimee Hirabayashi, Seattle's 10 middle schools have turned the corner from isolation and competition to collaborative networking. School leadership teams have begun to visit each other's schools. In March 2000, Seattle held its First Annual Middle Schools Conference, bringing all middle school teachers together to showcase best practice from schools and classrooms, teacher to teacher.

Some of the locations you want to visit may be a prohibitive distance for a road trip. Fortunately, the increasing prevalence of school and district Web sites makes it possible to make a virtual visit.

Consider Local Factors

Decisions in the school change process should involve new learning from both outside and inside the school. The previous two sections in this chapter provide the external focus of learning from research and best practice in other schools and districts. The emphasis in the next two sections is on learning about ourselves through analyzing each area of concern that gave rise to priority goals. The cause-and-effect diagram and force field analysis are tools that help sharpen perceptions and highlight assumptions that must be tested. The pie chart and pareto chart examples show how schools learned more about their own reality at this stage of digging further into the data. The last part of the chapter provides graphic organizers and a flowchart to examine instructional programs and coordinate district and school work on behalf of student achievement.

Cause-and-Effect Diagram (Fishbone)

A cause-and-effect diagram is a visual representation of the relationships between contributing factors and an issue or problem. Because the picture usually branches out like the skeleton of a fish, it has become known as a "fishbone."

Purpose. A cause-and-effect diagram is helpful when groups need to better understand why a problem situation exists and how it developed. This information can help teams identify the factors with the most impact and choose the most promising entry points for interventions.

When to Use. The cause-and-effect diagramming process is helpful when groups have agreed that a specific issue or problem should be the focus of planning and change. It can also be a useful tool in conflict management by providing greater understanding of elements that have contributed to the conflict situation.

Whom to Involve. Any of the shareholders who have been identified earlier may be involved in small groups to develop cause-and-effect diagrams and share their product and insights with others. In my experience, this group process is one uniquely suited to groups that include skeptics. The example that follows demonstrates how it can defuse some of their resistance by acknowledging that many of the causal factors are beyond the control of the school and can help shift their perspective from negatives to possibilities.

Materials Needed. Completing a cause-and-effect diagram is a simple paper-and-pencil process. If small groups will be reporting to a larger group, easel paper and markers should be used.

Tips for Facilitators

Explain to the group that before making snap decisions about how to solve a problem, participants need to be sure they understand it thoroughly. This activity will encourage looking back for causes before looking forward with plans. Have groups state the problem they are addressing in a simple phrase such as "student absenteeism" or "lack of problem-solving skills." The phrase should be written in a box (or the artistic may draw a fish head instead) halfway down the right-hand side of a large horizontal sheet of paper. A line should be drawn across the middle of the paper, like a spine leading to the head of the fish. As the group members brainstorm the factors that contribute to their concern, they write each one on a diagonal "bone" attached to the spine, or on a "barb" connected to a bone if it relates to a cause already mentioned.

Some formal group process handbooks emphasize that causal factors tend to fall into categories and that the categories should be identified first and bones attached to the appropriate category. For example, quality management fishbones often include the four categories of procedures, people, policies, and plant. Having seen too many groups get bogged down deciding what the categories should be, or arguing about which category a factor belongs with, I have left the process unstructured. It seems to be just as effective without the predetermined categories.

Some groups recognize their own categories after working a while and revise their fishbone accordingly.

A version of the quality improvement technique of "Ask why five times" can strengthen the fishbone exercise. When a contributing factor is identified, the repeated question "And where did that one come from?" or "And why is that?" can add more specificity to the analysis.

After the cause-and-effect diagram is drawn and discussed, guide the group to identify any follow-up steps. Factors over which the organization has no control may be acknowledged. There may be a need to gather more data on some of the factors, to see how much influence they actually have. Most important, the group should star or circle causes that it feels have great impact and that it is willing to address.

For Example: Absenteeism

Ten school leadership teams had been selected to participate in a 3-day workshop that would guide them through the process of developing a school improvement plan. They had been asked to bring student data and draft versions of any work they had already done on mission statements, goals, or action plans. It was fascinating to observe their approach to the day.

At one table sat a group of newspapers—at least, that's what it looked like. All I could see were the open sports sections of *USA Today* and local and state publications.

At another table, a group of early arrivals were poring over a stack of computer printouts, heedless even of the caterer's late delivery of the pastries. Heads together, the participants were engrossed in a discussion of which subtests matched their curriculum and mission closely enough to merit major attention as they set their improvement targets.

Another group entered carrying the lid of a copy paper box with waves of green-and-white-striped computer printouts spilling haphazardly over the edge. Locating the table with the school's name on it, the carrier dropped the box on the floor and used the side of his foot to slide it—none too gently—under the table out of sight. Having dispatched the data, this group attacked the coffee and doughnut table with much greater zeal. I overheard one say, "So what's with this woman we have to listen to about effective schools? Did someone report us defective?"

It was already shaping up to be one of those marvelous "opportunity days," like the tough games that some coaches refer to as character builders, when one of the speaker's companions approached me. "In all fairness, I really ought to let you know that there's no reason for us to be wasting 3 days at this workshop. We already have our school improvement plan done." Swallowing hard, I asked him to tell me what they had planned for the coming year. "Well, we got our biggest problem figured out. It's kids not coming to school. And we got two plans for working on it. First of all, we got a business partner that's going to donate us some equipment so we can program it to call those kids and get them going in the morning. Second of all, we got a committee all lined up to work on our attendance policy so these kids can't get by with skipping. Anything wrong with that?" By now I was *gulping* hard, but I managed to thank him for his honesty and suggested that they stick it out for at least this first day, listen carefully, and think about their plan, and we'd talk at the end of the day about whether their attendance at the next two would be worthwhile. "Well, I guess we might as well, we're already here."

During the first part of the morning, I shared some background on effective schools research with the group. When we did carousel brainstorming to record their impressions of the correlates identified by Edmonds and Lezotte, I praised this group for addressing attendance, linking it with orderly environment, high expectations for students, and opportunity to learn. I assured my new friend that his group was exactly right—kids aren't going to learn if they're not even there.

Later, I asked them to talk about whatever data they had available and what concerns emerged from this discussion or others that had already taken place at their school. This group repeated that their attendance data showed a need for improvement.

Lunch was provided in the room right next door, so I figured that this group would stick around for the afternoon. That's when we got to discuss how important it is to understand the problem we're addressing and know just what is causing it so we know where to begin changing it. The group in question began its fishbone of student absenteeism with "parents don't care" and went right on to list items such as "no transportation," "baby-sitting younger kids," "pretty low socio-economics," and "stay up too late at their night jobs." The other groups were getting along well, so I tried to coach this group a little. I commented, "You seem to have a pretty good handle on their family situation. Got any thoughts about the kids themselves?" The next phase started with "kids don't care either" and "unmotivated" (when they have night jobs?) and went on to "discipline problems," "low achievers," and "a couple of them are pregnant." About this time, I noticed one member of the group sort of digging around under the table, but it had a skirt around it and I didn't want to get too nosy, so I ignored him.

The work on the fishbone was bogging down, so I tried again. "It's really too bad some kids are like that, but I'm glad to see you're aware of them. Could there be any other source of factors that relate to whether kids come to school or not?" A soft voice from the other end of the table said, "Well, they don't like school when they do come." Several people just stared at her, so I reached over and wrote "don't like school" on a new bone. A few others added things such as "don't participate in anything," "can't see the point of learning," and "don't seem connected to anyone."

Just then, a head popped up with the copy paper box lid in his hand and an expression of amazement on his face. "Wait a minute. I've just been digging through here and it looks to me like there's about 20 kids or so in the whole school that are causing our absence rate to look so bad." My friend responded immediately. "Oh, yeah. So *who*?" As the analyst mentioned a name or two, other members of the group began to comment on the individuals. "Well, if ——— can just make it from the bus to the door without a fight, he does pretty well in class." "——— doesn't have any trouble getting here, but he's so interested in messing around the art room he doesn't follow his schedule." "If ——— wasn't so worried about her weight, she might have time to think about her work."

Because of a little data, the participants suddenly began to talk about students. And as they did, one brave soul said, "You know, if they are such low socio-economic status, do you think they'll have phones to call?" Another drew courage from that colleague and said, "If they really don't care about school, what good will a tougher attendance policy do?" My friend shrugged and said, "Well, maybe our plan isn't quite right, but look at the stuff on that fish thing. We can't do anything about that stuff."

FIGURE 5.1. Cause-and-Effect (Fishbone) Diagram of Student Absenteeism

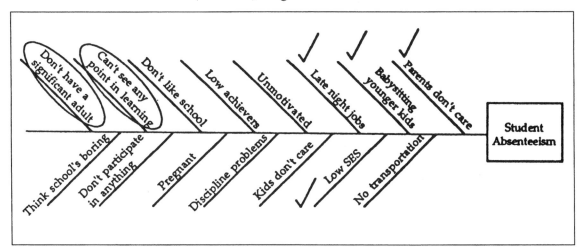

I was delighted and plunged right in. "You're right, you know. I have to agree with you that a lot of these things we can't control. Let's put a check mark by them. And then let's see what we can tackle."

Figure 5.1 shows the results. Not too many items got checked off because some members of the group began to argue that maybe the system *could* make some type of provisions for transportation and in-school child care. What they circled became the basis of a new action plan.

The next morning they got there first. By the end of the day, they had developed a plan to provide each of the chronic absentees with an adult in the school (teacher, custodian, or volunteer) who would check in with them each morning before school and follow up to see if they were taking work home afterward.

The next fall, I asked my contact in that district how the teams were getting along and what progress the members had made on their plans. "Well," he said, "they're all making progress, but only one school is really implementing what they talked about in June." It was the school that didn't want to be there.

Force Field Analysis

The cause-and-effect diagram helps groups identify the factors contributing to their problem or concern. Force field analysis goes a step further, looking at factors that work both for and against the desired result.

Purpose. Force field analysis is used to identify barriers that must be overcome and to focus on positive forces that can be mobilized for progress.

When to Use. A group may use force field analysis when it is considering a change effort. The results can help the members be more aware of barriers they didn't recognize. It can also increase a group's sense of efficacy by identifying advantages and possible allies that could help it succeed. Occasionally, time spent doing a force field analysis saves a group from investing time and effort when restraining forces so outweigh driving forces that it's clearly a lost cause from the outset.

Whom to Involve. All shareholders should feel welcome to participate directly or through their representatives on the leadership team or task force. It is particularly important to include those who were strong voices in identifying the issue or problem under consideration.

Materials Needed. Force field analysis is a paper-and-pencil exercise. Using easel paper and markers makes it easier to share the completed analysis with others.

Tips for Facilitators

Force field analysis is simply a structured version of brainstorming with a format provided for responses. The rules of brainstorming should be reviewed. Like the cause-and-effect diagram, it is important to push the participants beyond "filling in the blanks." They need to discuss and select which restraining forces they can minimize and which driving forces they will use to their advantage. From this discussion will emerge strategies that can be further developed as part of the action plan.

For Example: Year-Round School

An inner-city school team was concerned about the gap created in children's lives between May and September and had spent considerable time discussing and debating the value of year-round school. Most members agreed that it was a good concept but wondered if it was feasible to focus their school improvement efforts around restructuring the school calendar. They decided to complete a force field analysis and "calculate the odds" before going any further. Figure 5.2 shows their analysis.

After looking at it, they decided to work on summer provisions in collaboration with social service agencies and focus their grant funding toward those efforts. They concluded that their resources would get to children much quicker this way than by trying to influence the district, state, county, and parents in favor of year-round school.

Dig Into the Data

The "fishbone" story provides an example of how a more in-depth analysis of individual data can change the direction of a planning process. The next three examples share what school teams learned when they took a second look at data on instructional time, discipline problems, and the needs of homeless students. Pie charts and pareto charts can obviously be used in the initial School Portfolio. They are described in detail in this chapter because they provide such relevant examples of further study to guide the choice of strategies for change.

Pie Charts

A pie chart is a way to display data that is easy to understand and interpret. Like the histogram, it can be used in the initial School Portfolio to answer the "Where are we now?" question. It can also be used in a further study of local factors and added to the School Portfolio at that time.

FIGURE 5.2. Force Field Analysis for Year-Round School

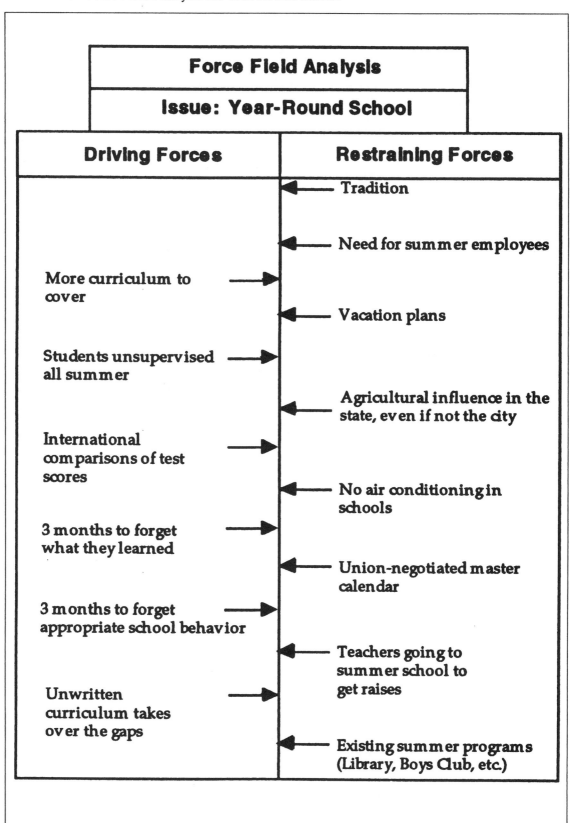

Purpose. The pie chart is particularly useful for demonstrating how a resource is used. Time, money, materials, and personnel are resources that must be used efficiently to help schools be as effective as possible in serving students and their communities.

When to Use. Pie charts can be useful to describe how a resource is apportioned for various uses. It can also show how students are divided into various groups, courses, or activities.

Whom to Involve. The important aspect of involvement with any use of data is that those who are part of the situation being analyzed are included in both gathering the information initially and then analyzing and interpreting it. When people are directly involved in collecting the data, they are much more likely to accept the results as an accurate representation of their situation.

Materials Needed. Developing the pie chart can easily be done by any individual using paper and pencil or software graphics.

Tips for Facilitators

Pie charts work best when there are a limited number of slices in the pie. If a resource is divided into so many uses that the pie has numerous slivers, the pie chart will not be as effective in delivering the information at a glance, and another type of graph or table should be used.

For Example: Instructional Time

The pie chart in Figure 5.3 illustrates the use of an important resource—instructional time. Students were observed in classrooms, and their behavior was tallied as interactive, noninteractive, and off-task. With few words of explanation, it is easy to see that students were actively engaged more than half the time but were passive receivers almost one third of the time and off task 13% of their time in class.

Pareto Charts

Pareto charts can be constructed to break down a major problem into more specific causes. School leaders then have a range of options to consider as they identify "where to start" to improve the situation.

Purpose. A pareto chart can be used when many factors are involved in a situation, and you need to know which to address first. A pareto chart is a form of vertical bar graph. Its unique feature is that it presents items in order of frequency so that a group can deal with "first things first."

When to Use. A pareto chart may be helpful after a survey or focus group has been conducted and a wide range of problems has been generated or recommendations have been proposed. A pareto chart can also display data on aspects of student behavior, such as various causes of student absences.

FIGURE 5.3. Pie Chart of Student Instructional Time Audit

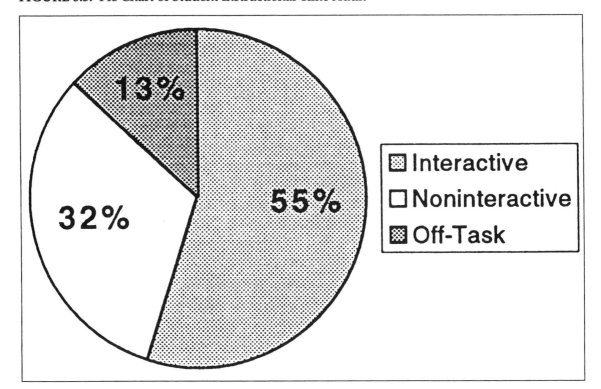

Whom to Involve. A pareto chart can be constructed by one person. Discussion of what the data mean and what to do about them should involve representatives of those who provided the data (such as survey respondents) and those who have responsibility for the factors described in the data.

Materials Needed. A pareto chart can be constructed using the data with paper and pencil or computer software.

Tips for Facilitators

Like any graph, a pareto chart has horizontal and vertical axes that must be clearly labeled. Sometimes data have identified a problem but provide no information on probable causes or related factors. It may be necessary to brainstorm what these causes or factors may be and gather another set of data. The results are displayed like a bar graph or histogram but with the factors placed in descending order of frequency.

In most cases, efforts toward improvement should begin with the factors that have the tallest bars. Common sense must prevail, however. If even a small percentage of cases are caused by some factor that is dangerous or may have legal ramifications, those situations must be addressed immediately.

For Example: Student Discipline

Staff members at one school were concerned about the number of students sent to the office for disciplinary reasons. They wondered whether student behav-

FIGURE 5.4. Pareto Chart of Student Discipline

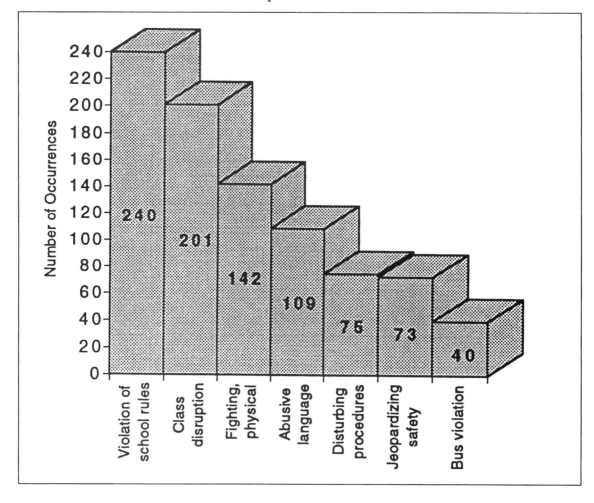

ior was getting worse, whether the offenses actually merited the principal's attention, and what relationship there might be to the new discipline policy that had been developed the summer before. They analyzed the reasons stated on the "pink slips" that students carried with them to the office and constructed the pareto chart in Figure 5.4.

First, they noticed that the greatest number of discipline referrals were related to violating school rules, outlined in their new policy. This discovery led them to reconsider the consequences in the policy and build in more responsibility at the classroom level before sending students out of the room. They also acknowledged that they could have been more conscientious about teaching the new rules to students and communicating them to parents.

The second bar on the pareto chart prompted a decision to provide classroom management training for teachers to help them be more proactive in preventing classroom disruptions in the first place. By the time they got to the third bar, they discovered that the cause they were most worried about (physical violence) was not the most frequent problem, and when they compared it with previous years, fighting had not increased at all.

Note that 880 discipline occurrences were analyzed altogether. Addressing just the first two causes would affect about half (441) of the incidents analyzed.

Without the pareto chart, the school staff might have worked hard to reduce fighting—certainly a valid effort—but with far less success at reducing the sheer number of students standing in line at the office.

For Example: Homeless Students

Teachers from a middle school in a deteriorating section of the city were attending a graduate course on total quality improvement. Their assignment was to work as a quality improvement team on a problem within their school. They had become concerned about the number of transient students who were housed in homeless shelters within their attendance area, and they decided to make that issue a focus of their study. Caring members of the staff had begun trying to find clothing for the students and made other efforts to help them but felt frustrated and overwhelmed. They didn't think that the school could function as a social service agency, but they were aware of the economic realities of these children.

To gather data for their project, the graduate students decided to conduct private interviews with the homeless students who were now attending the school to find out what they most wanted. They particularly anticipated responses such as clothing and social acceptance and feared that they would get data that they would not be able to do anything about. When they came to the next class, they were carrying a pareto chart and wearing expressions of amazement and chagrin. The tallest bar on their pareto chart identified a perceived need for security guards. These students had moved away from a major inner-city area where crime was rampant, and they felt insecure in an environment that did not have guards as a visible presence. The second-tallest bar amazed them. These homeless students indicated that they needed the school to provide "help with our class work" much more than any of the things the adults thought they would want. Teachers who had been saying, "We're a school, we're here to teach, we can't be a social service agency" discovered that kids felt the same way. They wanted to be taught. The quality improvement project shifted focus from "We're not social workers" to "How can we quickly diagnose their skill levels and provide basic instruction that will move them forward, even if they are with us only a short time?"

Analyze Current Practice

Earlier in this chapter, I listed the study of best practices as an essential step in preparation for making decisions for school change. Unfortunately, too many school leaders and shareholders learn about best practice, nod and say, "Oh, we do that," pat each other on the back, and carry on the status quo—without actually knowing what instructional programs and practice really look like within their schools. Specialized models, such as curriculum mapping, can capture the written curriculum. Less formal, more personal approaches are needed to understand the taught curriculum and the instructional methods in common use. Many of the tools already introduced can be adapted for this purpose. For example, the focus group strategy can be used in grade level, department, and interdisciplinary groups to compare current practice with best practice. One way of synthesizing research and best practice, and using it as a tool to analyze current practice, is to develop a graphic organizer.

Graphic Organizers

A graphic organizer is simply a drawing or diagram that helps organize thoughts or see the components and relationships within a complex problem or situation. Figure 2.1, which illustrates the relationship of the five guiding questions to the stages of school change, is an example of a graphic organizer. It provides a common focus to tie together the parts of this book, so that the reader can turn to it when wondering, "Now where does *this* fit?"

Purpose. A graphic organizer is designed to illustrate complex relationships. It is also a powerful way to synthesize pages of text into a one-page reference guide.

When to Use. Teachers often develop *advance* organizers to introduce a new topic of study and help students anticipate what they will be learning. In a similar way, a school study group may develop a graphic organizer to share what they have learned with the rest of the staff. It's a visual tool that does not require a lot of reading to highlight the main points. A wise senior management team might stop in the middle of a school year and say, "Whoa, how many new initiatives have we already begun, and how are they related?" Team members might need to draw a picture to explain it to themselves and then be able to improve communication with shareholders.

Whom to Involve. With most group process activities, we know who should be included by asking who is affected by the outcome. Developing a graphic organizer may be unique in the need for participation by individuals who have expert knowledge and are in a position to be able to see the big picture. For example, the graphic organizers in Figures 5.5, 5.6, and 5.7 were developed in groups led by curriculum consultants who were experts in their disciplines. Figure 5.8 was developed from my perspective as an outside consultant, having worked in multiple roles at both the school and central office level.

Materials Needed. The sky's the limit of how elaborate graphic organizers can become through the use of technology. But all that's needed initially is paper, pencil, and analytical thinking.

Tips for Facilitators

Develop the graphic organizer with a group if you have one that includes the expert knowledge and systems thinking that you need. This isn't always possible. Sometimes you need to do your own sketching and then have it reviewed by a group or several individuals before you introduce it as a group process tool.

If you are leading a study group, the components of the graphic organizer may come from various sources. Persons or subgroups report what they learned and contribute where they think it belongs in the big picture. One way to synthesize a jigsaw cooperative learning activity is for the home group to develop a graphic organizer of what it learned.

(text continues on page 82)

FIGURE 5.5. Graphic Organizer: Essential Components of a Reading Program

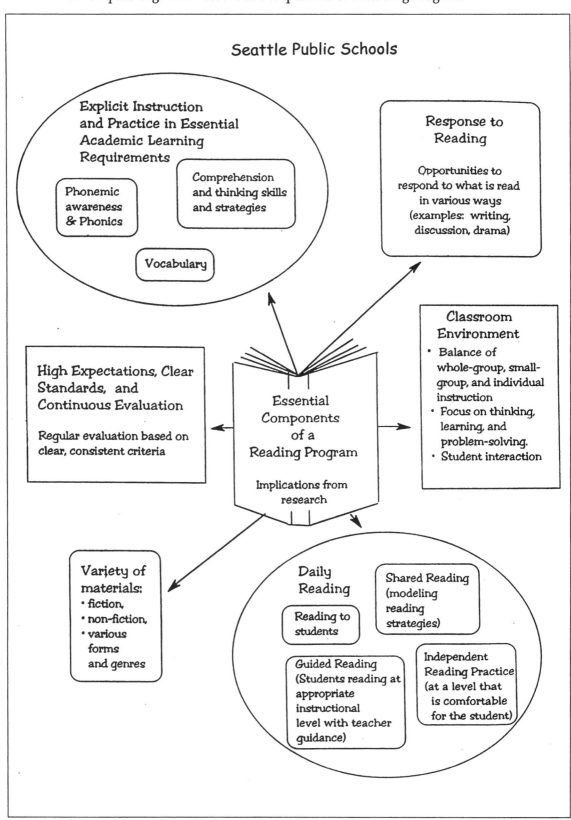

FIGURE 5.6. Graphic Organizer: Essential Components of a Writing Program

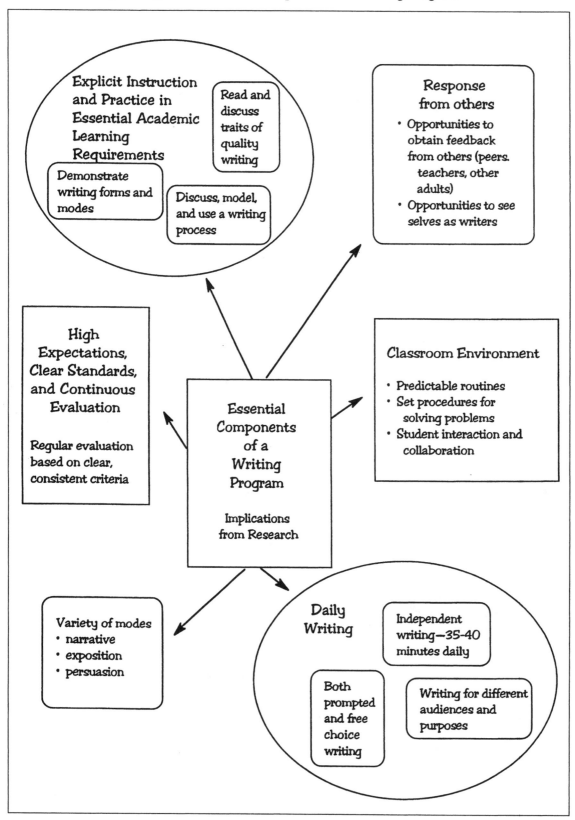

FIGURE 5.7. Graphic Organizer: Essential Components of a Mathematics Program

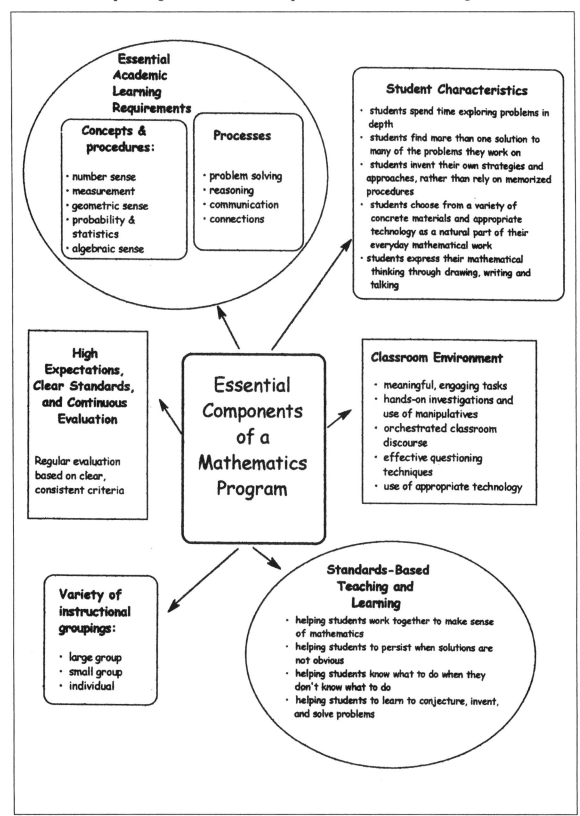

FIGURE 5.8. Using Student Performance Data to Integrate District Curriculum Work With School Improvement

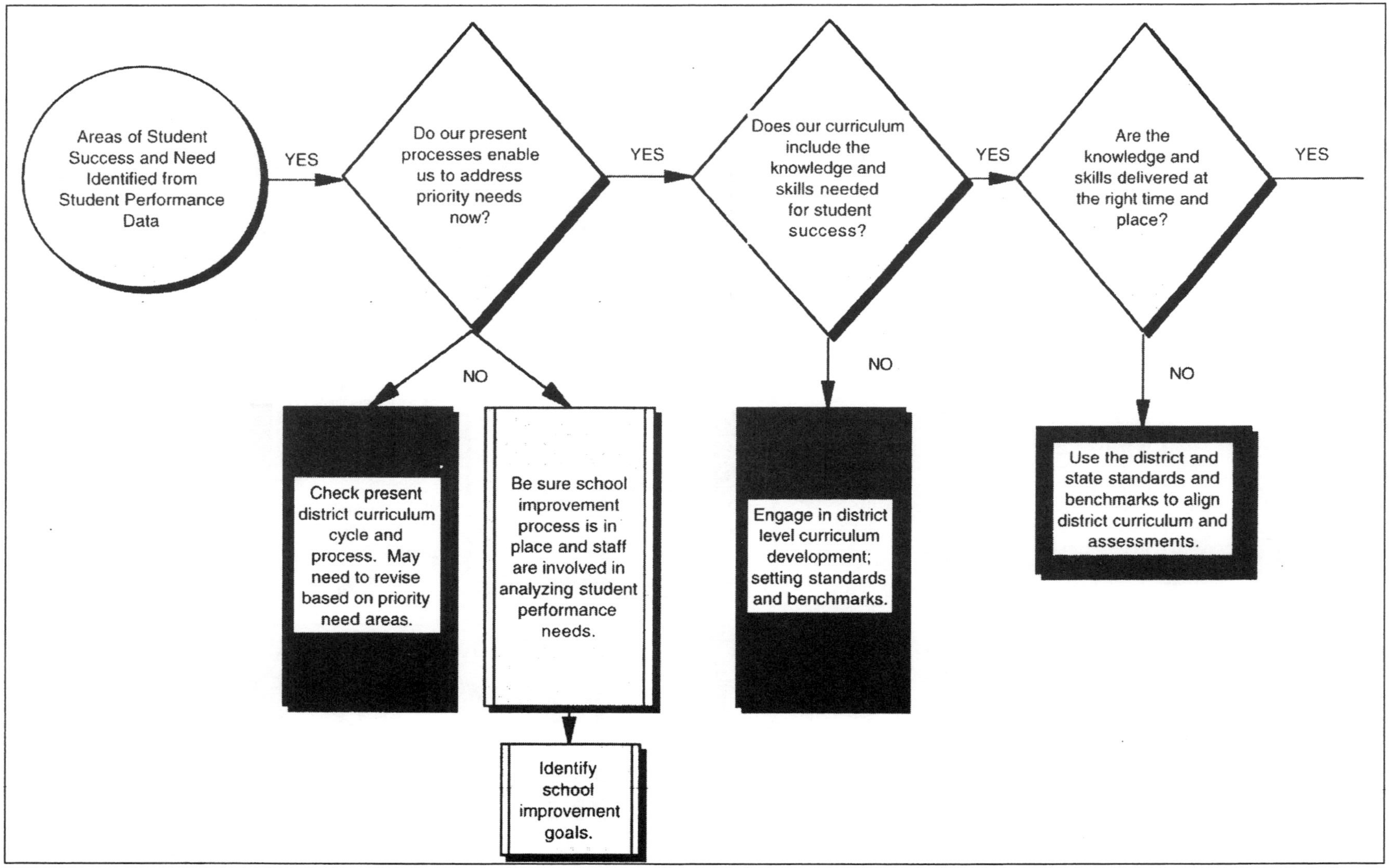

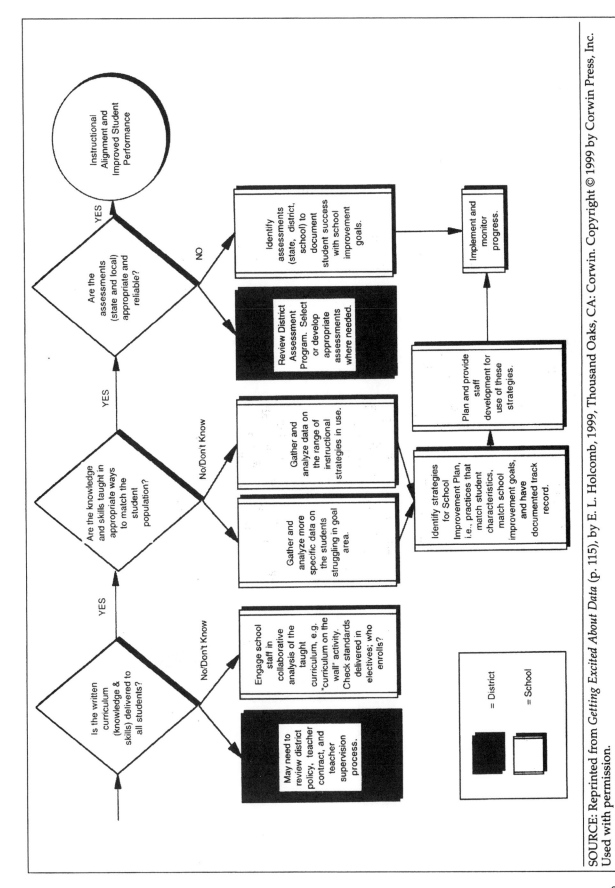

Instructional Alignment and Improved Student Performance

Are the assessments (state and local) appropriate and reliable?

Are the knowledge and skills taught in appropriate ways to match the student population?

Is the written curriculum (knowledge & skills) delivered to all students?

YES

YES

YES

NO

No/Don't Know

No/Don't Know

Identify assessments (state, district, school) to document student success with school improvement goals.

Review District Assessment Program. Select or develop appropriate assessments where needed.

Gather and analyze data on the range of instructional strategies in use.

Gather and analyze more specific data on the students struggling in goal area.

Engage school staff in collaborative analysis of the taught curriculum, e.g. "curriculum on the wall" activity. Check standards delivered in electives; who enrolls?

May need to review district policy, teacher contract, and teacher supervision process.

Identify strategies for School Improvement Plan, i.e., practices that match student characteristics, match school improvement goals, and have documented track record.

Plan and provide staff development for use of these strategies.

Implement and monitor progress.

= District

= School

SOURCE: Reprinted from *Getting Excited About Data* (p. 115), by E. L. Holcomb, 1999, Thousand Oaks, CA: Corwin. Copyright © 1999 by Corwin Press, Inc. Used with permission.

For Example: The Three Rs

What do you do when you have had several years of successive cuts in curriculum and instruction staff, coinciding with emphasis on site-based planning and budgeting, and now a state accountability system prompts the school board to ask how reading is taught in the schools? What do you do when aggregated test scores show the public that overall improvement in student achievement is occurring across the district, but you also know that some schools are struggling and some are even declining? The challenge is to find out what's being done—and not being done—and assist schools, without violating the culture of site-based autonomy and without starting a war over the "one best way" (such as the example later in this chapter).

Reading specialist Joan Dore figured it out. She needed a way to condense all the research she knew about balanced reading programs into something visual, nonthreatening, and easy to talk about with individuals and groups of teachers. She knew that every school was doing at least part of the puzzle well, but many were missing important pieces. She wanted to value what every school and teacher was doing but stretch their awareness and build the rest of a comprehensive reading program in every school. So she drew a picture of the essential components of a reading program (Figure 5.5). As the district embarks on a major literacy initiative, this graphic organizer guides the diagnosis of each school's practices and serves as a reference point for professional development. As new instructional strategies are introduced, external trainers, internal consultants, administrators, and teachers can point to this organizer and say, "We're learning this because it fits *here* and will strengthen *this* part of our reading program."

Joan's graphic organizer for reading was so well received that teachers asked for similar examples for writing and mathematics. Charlotte Carr and Allison Harris developed Figures 5.6 and 5.7 to stimulate professional dialogue and analyze current practice in their disciplines as well. Does that mean that every school now has the same instructional programs and methods? No. It does mean that—whatever they call it, however they schedule and staff for it—they must describe how all the components are present in the opportunities they provide for children.[1]

Partner With Your District

This heading may seem self-evident, but it's tragic how many schools see the district as an enemy rather than as a partner. School districts need to frame their work as support services to the schools, and schools need to know how to access the services that are available. The flowchart in Figure 5.8 was developed to answer the anguished question raised in Scenario 5 in Chapter 2. When student performance data identify an area of need, a series of questions guides both district and school work.

For example, Washington State's standards include five strands of math concepts and procedures: number sense, measurement, geometric sense, algebraic sense, and statistics and probability. Let's say that state assessment results indicated that students performed quite well in number sense and measurement but poorly in the other three strands.

The first question on the flowchart prompts discussion at both levels, to be sure that both district curriculum work and the school improvement plan will focus on the need. The second and third questions ask whether geometric sense, algebraic sense, and statistics and probability are included in the curriculum—and at what level—and must be answered for the district as a whole. Teacher representatives would participate in necessary revision, but this task should not have to occur simultaneously and independently at every school.

The district, however, can only provide the aligned curriculum and materials. It's the school that must determine whether all strands of the math curriculum are delivered to students and whether teachers are skilled in the methods that will reach their students. If additional teaching strategies are needed, the school's improvement plan would include professional development provisions to meet the need.

The assessment question resides at both levels. State and district decisions govern the large-scale assessments that are administered to all students. Schools use data from those assessments in their decision making and also make decisions about the types of classroom evidence that they will collect and the indicators of progress that they will monitor as they work toward their goals (see Chapter 6).

Select Strategies

As I wrote this section, I could see the Horsetooth, a rock formation on the front range of the Colorado Rockies. To get from here to Estes Park and over the top to Granby, there is really only one route, the Trail Ridge Road. But the view from the deck in back is different. The high plains stretch as far as the eye can see. To get from here to Minneapolis, there are several routes. Having a clear destination does not complete the planning. If there are many possible routes, choices must be made that will get the most people on board and headed in the same direction.

Decision Matrix

Purpose. A decision matrix is used to help groups reach consensus on the best solution to a complex issue or problem. Choosing criteria that would define an appropriate strategy helps participants focus on common values. Brainstorming all possible solutions brings out greater creativity and can counteract the "only one right or best way" thinking that is so prevalent.

When to Use. A decision matrix is helpful when multiple strategies have been suggested, especially if there are intense feelings about several of them. It should definitely be used when organizations have a history of simply adopting the latest innovation and assuming that it will match their needs, or when they show little evidence of connecting their data and their value system to decision making. Use of the decision matrix should have been preceded by study of the organization's own data ("Where are we now?") and study of best practices for achieving the results desired ("Where do we want to go?").

Whom to Involve. Group processes should be open for participation. When using a decision matrix, it is particularly important to include those who are most affected by the current situation and those who will be most responsible for implementing the chosen strategies.

Materials Needed. Chart paper and markers will be needed for the first two steps. Each participant will need a copy of the decision matrix. There are two ways of providing this. Blank copies of the matrix form can be distributed, and as the possible solutions and criteria are generated, each participant can fill them in. Another method is to complete the lists of solutions and criteria, enter them on a laptop computer, and print the matrix during a break. The three steps of listing solutions, setting criteria, and ranking the possibilities may even occur on different occasions.

Tips for Facilitators

Engage the group in a review of what was learned in answer to the "Where are we now?" and "Where do we want to go?" questions. Summarize what has been learned by study groups who have researched best practice to achieve the desired results.

Divide the large group into smaller groups or table teams and have them list all the possible strategies that might be employed to accomplish the goal or address the concern they have identified. As with brainstorming, encourage participants to generate as many variations and solutions as they can. Allow brief periods of wait time to stimulate more divergent thinking. Save the lists from all groups.

After a break or at another session within a few days, have the groups shift into a more reflective mode. Review the mission or belief statements that identify their core values. Ask them to consider what criteria would describe an ideal solution. List these criteria.

The decision matrix is constructed by listing the suggested changes or strategies along the left side of a grid. The criteria for a good decision become headings across the top.

To use the matrix, have participants go down each column and give each suggested solution a rating from 1 to 5, with 5 representing those suggestions that most closely fit the criterion heading for that column. Repeat this with each column. Participants can add the ratings across each row to get a total value for each of the suggested strategies. Their individual ratings can then be used in a whole group exercise, such as nominal group process or weighted voting.

For Example: The Reading Debate

The elementary school team had reviewed test data and determined that one area of focus should be on improving reading achievement. Deciding how to accomplish this goal awoke a history of conflict between the "phonicians" and the "whole languagers." The progress that had been made to heal wounds and strengthen the school culture was at risk because staff members were approaching the goal of improved reading achievement as an either/or proposition. The facilitator had difficulty getting more than those two possible solutions generated in the first attempt at this process and had to temporarily abandon it.

Instead, the group put solutions on hold and began to generate criteria that would characterize a good solution. The members agreed that an acceptable solution

◆ Would be consistent with their mission and beliefs

◆ Would help staff work together, not be divided

◆ Would include a component of parent participation

◆ Could be implemented with existing resources

As members focused on these criteria, they began to realize that neither phonics nor whole language, in and of itself, contained all these elements. More ideas emerged for the "possible solutions" list, and they were able to construct their decision matrix. They realized that they had rejected a third program (Success for All) because they lacked the resources for full implementation of this labor-intensive approach. At the same time, they discovered that there were aspects of the model that they could adapt to their situation. What resulted was a unique approach that alternated days between whole language activities and cross-grade flexible skill grouping similar to the Joplin plan (which was one of the foundations of the Success for All design). They also discovered that parent volunteers could be readily engaged in whole language activities, freeing teachers for more intense skill work with students. By focusing on their criteria, they invented their own creative solutions that in turn created a stronger sense of commitment.

A Variation: Perplexed About Portables

Another school was challenged by increasing enrollment and the district's decision to remedy overcrowding through the use of portable classrooms. Initial discussions about who or what should be housed in the portable classrooms were rapidly becoming characterized by discussions of seniority and comments such as "I've taught in this room for 22 years, and I have only 3 more to go, and you'd have to carry me out in a coffin before I'd give up my room." As each grade level was listed for potential location in the portables, the objections changed from "They're too small to be wandering from one building to another; they might get lost" to "They're too big to be wandering from one building to another; they'll disrupt everything." The list of possible solutions then shifted to "special" programs. They were all written down, despite objections such as "How can you have art without a sink?" and "Why have the traffic of all 500+ kids going back and forth when there's only a need for three or four classrooms?" and "You can't put the computer lab there because it would be too easy to break into."

Although the facilitator ignored the comments and objections when recording all the possible solutions, he reintroduced them during the discussion of criteria for a good decision. "I understand that security from break-ins is important. Do you want that as a criterion?" It was included, along with others such as "least number of students moving" and "should fit program needs." As the criteria were identified, a whole new solution was introduced. Two teachers had wanted to try team teaching, but their rooms were too far apart, and they had been afraid of the noise and hall traffic exchanging students. This suggestion started a whole new line of thought, and two primary teachers mentioned that they had been interested in multiage classrooms but hadn't thought too much about it because they were so crowded. The resulting decision was to use one portable for team teaching and one as a multiage primary unit. Not only did the school solve its "who gets the portables?" problem, but it also had an opportunity to introduce two new instructional settings that had never been tried before because the interested teachers had been "locked into" their existing spaces.

Plan the Journey

A common characteristic of school improvement plans that never happen is that they identify strategies they will use (cooperative learning, a self-esteem program, multiple intelligences) without analyzing what implementation of those strategies will entail. Any one of the strategies mentioned represents many substeps needed to provide training and support for implementation. When schools identify popular topics such as multiple intelligences and learning styles, their plans often involve training in the content knowledge without sufficient consideration of changes that would need to be made in the school itself to reflect those concepts. Although plans will surely be adjusted during implementation, they must be sufficiently developed to clearly describe the magnitude of change they require and the demands they will place on people, time, and budgets.

Action Planning

Purpose. An action plan is developed to lay out the specific steps that will be required to put a new strategy or program into place. Answering the question "How will we get there?" identified some "what's" (the strategies). Answering the "Where do we want to go?" question included focus on the belief system of the organization as "why." Action planning helps a group work out the "who, when, where, and how."

When to Use. An action plan should be developed after the organization has set priorities for improvement, studied practices and programs that have been effective, and chosen the approaches best suited to their goals and school context.

Whom to Involve. Because an action plan needs to identify specific steps, timelines, and resources, it is important to involve people who have information about and access to the school calendar and budget and who have a big picture perspective of all that is occurring in the organization. School teams often find it helpful to include a central office support person in the action-planning stage. If a major innovation such as multiage classrooms is being implemented, it is advisable to invite a consultant or a team member from another school that is already using the approach. These resource persons can provide advice on how they approached the change and even more valuable insights about problems they didn't anticipate and what they might have done to avoid them.

The specificity required in action planning often brings the realization that the strategy or approach to be used is a much more complex change than it first appeared. In some situations, it is helpful to identify major subtasks and assign a small group to develop that part of the action plan. For example, a major change such as multiage classrooms needs a component of parent education and communication. Involvement of parents in this planning subgroup is essential.

Materials Needed. Chart paper, markers, and large stick-on notes are commonly used for drafting an action plan as a group. The plan can then be typed on a laptop computer and printed for everyone to review. Once it is in the computer, it can readily be revised as it is adjusted throughout implementation.

Tips for Facilitators

Formats for school improvement plans can be found in many of the resources listed in the annotated bibliography. Some action plans are developed in chart form, and others are written in narrative form. The common elements are steps to be taken, who will be involved, who will be responsible, resources needed, time required and schedule, and indicators of completion or progress. A simple way to begin is by using these elements as column headings on a large bulletin board or wall. The sequence of development is "work all the way down, and then across." In other words, first list all the steps that need to be taken. As facilitator, repeatedly ask, "And what else does that involve?" This helps the group break down major tasks into their component parts. Another common question to ask is "What would need to happen before that?" This question guides the group to identify missing steps and create a sequence.

The group will continually recognize missing steps and rearrange the sequence of tasks, which can make messy recording for the facilitator. Writing each task on a large stick-on note makes moving them around and inserting new ones neat and easy.

When the sequence of steps or tasks seems complete, the group works across the chart horizontally for each step. Have the group identify the person responsible for each step and the people who will participate. Discuss whether there is a budgetary consideration. As the group moves to the timeline column, remind them that "time is money." If released time is going to be provided, there will be substitute costs. If compensation for time must be provided, that cost needs to be estimated. Timelines should consider the school calendar and capitalize on any staff development days or inservice time to fit with the school's action plan for improvement.

A most neglected but essential column is the last column, often given the heading of monitoring or evaluation. Too often, this column is simply used to check off completion of the activity, for example, "All staff attended a workshop on cooperative learning." This is inadequate because it does not assess whether anyone actually went back to the classroom and applied the knowledge and skills that were learned in the workshop. The example of brainstorming used in Chapter 4 generated observable indicators that distinguish the behavior of lifelong learners. The criteria that will be observed or measured must be identified at the time the action plan is developed to ensure that progress can be reported as results achieved, not just steps taken (see Chapter 6).

For Example: Mentors for Chronic Absentees

Earlier in this chapter, the group process technique of cause-and-effect (fishbone) diagramming was introduced with the example of a school leadership team that changed from revising an attendance policy to creating one-to-one mentor relationships between chronic absentees and caring adults in the school environment. Figure 5.9 shows the action plan developed by the team to implement that new approach.

Note

1. Joan Dore, Charlotte Carr, and Allison Harris can be contacted by e-mail (jdore@seattleschools.org, ccarr@seattleschools.org, and aharris@seattleschools.org).

FIGURE 5.9. Action Plan for Mentor Program

School: Anytown Middle School School Year(s): 1995-96

Improvement Objective: To improve student attendance

Members of Team or Task Force:

M. Black   M. Green
J. White   J. Jackson
B. Brown

Strategy: Develop 1:1 student-adult mentor relationships for chronic absentees

Rationale: Research findings indicate that student engagement and personal bonding with adults in the school are related to attendance and achievement

Activities: Steps to Be Taken	Persons Responsible	Persons Involved	Resources Needed	Timeline	Monitoring, Evaluation
Develop criteria to identify the chronic absentees	Counselors	SIT Subcommittee	Part of June workshop time	During June workshop	Criteria approved by SIT at August meeting
List the students who need to be involved	Counselor on SIT	Homeroom teachers	—	During June workshop	Presented and approved by SIT at August meeting

(continued)

FIGURE 5.9. Continued

Activities: Steps to Be Taken	Persons Responsible	Persons Involved	Resources Needed	Timeline	Monitoring, Evaluation
Set expectations for students who participate	Counselor on SIT	Homeroom teachers	—	During June workshop	Presented and approved by SIT at August meeting
Notify parents and get permission to contact students	Counselor	Counseling secretary	—	Before registration in August	Parent permissions returned
Set expectations for adult mentors	SIT subcommittee chair	SIT subcommittee	—	During June workshop	Approval by SIT at August meeting
Develop training for mentors	Assistant principal/staff development coordinator	SIT subcommittee/ homeroom teachers	Food for picnic	July	Approval by SIT at August meeting
Recruit and select mentors	Assistant principal	Homeroom teachers	—	July and August	List of mentors

Match students to mentors	Assistant principal	Counselors	—	July and August	List of possible matches
Hold mentor training and gain commitment	Assistant principal/staff development coordinator	Mentors/homeroom teachers	Stipends for 2-hour training sessions ($1,250) (25 mentors @ $50)	August	Mentors sign commitment forms
Hold meeting of students and mentors or make individual contact with students	Counselors/ assistant principal	Students/mentors/ homeroom teachers	—	August	Students return commitment forms
Determine times and places that mentors will contact students	Mentors	Students	—	First week of school	Schedules turned in to assistant principal

(continued)

FIGURE 5.9. Continued

Activities: Steps to Be Taken	Persons Responsible	Persons Involved	Resources Needed	Timeline	Monitoring, Evaluation
Schedule and hold mentor meetings	Assistant principal	Counselors/mentors/homeroom teachers	Early release time once per month	Monthly, October–May	Minutes of meetings/summary of student attendance and grades
Reexamine attendance data	Counselors	—	—	Weekly by student; monthly for all	Graph attendance and grades each month as run charts
Plan celebration for mentors and students	Assistant principal	Students/mentors/families/homeroom teachers	Budget for food, certificates, etc.	May	Progress certificates to students with % improvement

6

Answering the "How Will We Know We Are (Getting) There?" Question

It seemed as if all my friends were going to exotic places that year. One group went to the Caribbean on spring break. Others were taking summer vacations in Europe. A couple were going through the selection process for overseas teaching with the Department of Defense. All of them had invited me to come along, but I couldn't seem to muster much enthusiasm. Some recalcitrant part of me kept saying, "There are so many wonderful things to see in our own country. When I've done all the states, I'll start in on the world."

That made me curious about how many states I had already visited and which ones I still needed to see. On impulse, I bought a child's cardboard puzzle with each state outline forming a piece, and I glued on all the ones I'd been to as a child on family vacations or as an adult. I was amazed to discover that there were only 17 left, and most of them were in the Northeast. So while my friends planned for Europe, I planned for New England. I didn't want to be locked in with too tight a schedule to explore, but I did want my route laid out, so I had AAA prepare a Triptik for me. A Triptik is a set of maps about the size of a shopping list pad that's bound at the top with a coil. It's easy to hold and read while driving. Each page represents somewhere between 100 and 200 miles. For 3½ weeks, I marked my progress by the number of pages flipped in my Triptik. When I got home, I celebrated my accomplishments by gluing 13 more state pieces onto my puzzle.

The journey of school improvement is much like that, although an organization rarely reaches a state of completion as visible as the completed map of the United States. There will always be more destinations to pursue. Motivation has to come from proof of progress, because perfection will never be attained.

In previous chapters, we explored three of the critical questions of school improvement. The first was "Where are we now?" which required us to look carefully at the culture of our organization and at the performance of our students. Use of data was important in that answer. The second question was "Where do we want to go?" To set a clear goal, it was important to define the characteristics or observable indicators of the desired state in contrast to the status quo. The third question was "How will we get there?" Development of action plans required us to identify behaviors and results that can be observed or measured to demonstrate our progress (see "Indicators" on Figure 2.1).

If those first three phases were completed carefully, answering the question "How will we know we are getting there?" should be fairly straightforward. Knowing whether we are getting there simply means doing what we said we would do in our plan and checking what we said we would check. That's like the D (do) and the C (check) of the PDCA quality improvement cycle (see Figure 1.1). In the RPTIM model, it is the I and the M. Wood used the I for implementation and the M to stand for maintenance. I believe M must also stand for monitoring as it does in the Three Is. Unless the progress of implementation is monitored, institutionalization may never occur. There's a lot of truth in the aphorism that "what gets measured gets done." There's also truth in the flip side—that what *doesn't* get measured or monitored often *doesn't* get done. It's just so easy to let things slide if they have no deadlines or checkpoints.

On Figure 2.1, the question "How will we know we are getting there?" is posed above the box labeled "Indicators." The two bullets in the "Indicators" box represent two types of monitoring that must occur. The first is **indicators of implementation.** Most of us have seen posters with the slogan "Plan Your Work—Work Your Plan." This chapter raises the question "Are you working your plan?" and discusses the importance of making sure the strategies that were chosen are actually being used. No new practice can become part of "how we do things around here" (institutionalization) until it has moved from planning and training into consistent, skilled implementation.

The other bullet in the "Indicators" box represents evidence of progress toward the desired results. These are called **indicators of impact.** Once you have a plan, and know you are working the plan, it's time to ask the toughest question: "Is your plan working?" The overarching purpose of school improvement is to improve student performance. The time, energy, and commitment for change will be misplaced if the change is not clearly linked to greater effectiveness with students.

The "How will we know we are getting there?" question is also represented by the second "How?" above the oval labeled "mission." It reminds us that a mission statement isn't something that we write, print, and file. It's a living document that captures organizational values. These values should surface and ground every substantive discussion on every major decision.

I recently attended a seminar on high school reform. A panel of principals and teachers took turns describing their schools' demographics and settings and reasons for starting down the path of change. In a second round of comments, each speaker outlined the particular changes each school made and how the staff went about the decision-making process. Knowing how complex high school change is, the audience took copious notes and applauded every presenter. But during the break, the main question in the halls and rest room (ladies', anyway) was this: "So-and-so went on and on about the Coalition of Essential Schools' principles and how their main goal was to personalize education, but then they said they voted to increase their schedule to an eight-period day. How can they think that more, shorter class periods will personalize education?" We all understood that much is left unsaid when a speaker has only two 3-minute presentations, so there may be an appropriate answer to the question. The point of the example is that those who watch and listen to our work in schools are checking whether the actions we take match the rhetoric we speak. As you'll learn later in this chapter, Nathan Hale High School applied the principle of personalization in quite a different way.

Are We Working Our Plan?

In Chapter 5, we met a team of middle school teachers who were concerned about attendance. They began with a "crack down on absentees" attitude and planned to communicate electronically with their homes and to develop a more stringent attendance policy. But a more precise look at their data prompted discussion of individual students, and they refocused their energy on a plan to match each chronic absentee with an adult mentor. Their analysis was illustrated in Figure 5.1, and their plan was featured as Figure 5.9. This action plan includes a column called "Monitoring, Evaluation" that identifies the evidence that will show goals being met. This evidence should contain indicators of implementation and indicators of impact. Figure 5.9 shows that the initial steps involve planning, training, and implementation, so the implementation indicators are items such as criteria approved, parent permissions returned, lists of mentors and students, commitment forms, and schedules. These documents are kept on file. If this project were grant funded, they would be part of the grant evaluation. They demonstrate that the adults are "working their plan."

For Example: Indicators of Standards-Based Teaching and Learning

Washington State is one of 49 states with education reform legislation that identifies state standards (essential academic learning requirements) and mandates a statewide performance assessment system. Because the tests in reading, writing, communication, and math are given at 4th, 7th, and 10th grades, the state standards have benchmarks at those three levels to provide the test specifications. Beyond that, an understanding of what needs to be taught and when is left up to districts and schools.

The Seattle School District already had a long history of curriculum work, so it was imperative to implement the state standards by building on and integrating the curriculum frameworks and other previous projects. More than 300 teachers were engaged in a Standards Network to backward map from the state benchmark levels and clarify the benchmarks for the intervening grades. Many districts do this initial work, but too often the result is another notebook of objectives that sits atop the vinyl monument of curriculum projects past and present.

Seattle took two steps further so there would be indicators of implementation and impact. One step was identification of the characteristics of standards-based teaching and learning that should emerge in schools and classrooms. The other step was to develop classroom-based assessments that reflect the format and level of challenge of the state tests, pilot them, and develop anchor papers and scoring guides directly from the work of our own students in Seattle schools. We believed that the best way to understand what a standard really demands is to see how it looks from the assessment end of the instructional cycle.

The 15 Indicators of Standards-Based Teaching and Learning are presented in Figure 6.1. This list of characteristics has been used in many ways. For example, they were introduced to principals in breakout sessions at a principals' retreat 4 months before the standards and benchmarks were even taken to the school board for adoption. Principals were asked to discuss each indicator and informally rate their schools on a loosely defined scale:

4—Fully implemented by all teachers

3—Mostly in place

2—Off to a good start

1—Still catching on

Through a simple show of hands, we tallied their ratings, and participants observed which indicators were already in evidence and could be used as a foundation for next steps. We also noticed which indicators were least in evidence across all schools. This helped us focus our staff development plans for the coming year.

In addition to the use of the 15 Indicators in training workshops and videos, principals have used this set of characteristics to develop implementation plans for their individual schools. They were not given a required timeline but were asked to work with their staff to develop an implementation plan for Seattle's standards-based learning system. Principals also used the 15 Indicators as a reference for formative discussions with individual teachers.

For Example: John Hay Elementary School

When the leadership team from John Hay Elementary School[1] presented their academic achievement plan for review, they included this report of implementation indicators.

Summary of School-Wide Standards Roll-Out—1999-2001

Classroom Implementation

> ► Visible posting of standards within the classroom and on hallway bulletin boards

> ► Grade level/teacher calendars of standards covered, submitted to Principal and shared with grade level teams

> ► Use of Classroom-Based Assessments to include in first year: (1) At least one CBA for each strand of math, scored jointly by grade level teams and results reported back to Math Goal Team for school-wide data share, (2) Use of all reading and writing CBAs in every classroom, (3) Use of reading assessment note-

FIGURE 6.1. Indicators of Standards-Based Teaching and Learning

1. The district has developed clear statements of what students should know and be able to do.

2. Standards apply to all students with high expectations for their success.

3. The teacher knows how each lesson relates to district and state academic standards.

4. Students know what they are learning, what standards are related to it, and why they are learning it.

5. Standards are constant; instructional strategies and time are the variables.

6. Planning begins with standards rather than materials.

7. Practice activities are clearly aligned to standard(s) with the student as worker and the teacher as coach.

8. Students know how the teacher expects them to show what they've learned.

9. Students frequently evaluate their own work before the teacher does, using the same criteria.

10. Feedback to students is related to performance levels on standards, not based on comparison with other students.

11. Student performance data are used to revise curriculum and instruction.

12. The assessment system includes a balance of external tests for program evaluation and classroom assessments for individual student diagnosis and instruction.

13. Students have multiple opportunities to demonstrate achievement of standards.

14. Assessment of student achievement is consistent across teachers and schools, using common performance indicators.

15. Teachers work with colleagues to share and compare scoring of classroom-based assessments.

books utilizing at least two strategies from Bonnie Campbell
Hill training in August 1999

► Lesson plans include identification of targeted standards AND
  benchmarks

► Identification of and early intervention for students in lowest
  achieving ranges of assessments

► Early K-2 reading/literacy focus with concentration on standards and reading continuum progress

► Math journals done in every class with writing emphasis on de-
  fending solutions to problems

► Visits to each other's classrooms or other school classrooms that
  are scoring well on Washington Assessment of Student Learning

► Bi-monthly newsletters home to parents with emphasis upon
  curriculum and standards familiarity

School-Wide Implementation

► Curriculum Night presentations focused upon explanation of
  standards and assessments

► Development of report card alternative by Leadership team
  members and principal (Standards Student Report) for first tri-
  mester conference

► Emphasis upon standards in every parent/teacher conference
  to include: (1) New written Standards Student Report, (2) sharing of District standards booklet, and (3) sharing of at least two
  pieces of student work as compared against scoring guides and
  anchor papers

► Principal communication about standards in bi-monthly Principal Page newsletters as well as letter home regarding standards
  integration with parent/teacher conferences

► Use of Boeing Grant of $10,000 to further training in areas of
  scoring student work, using data effectively to formulate goals,
  visiting out of district classrooms using the state standards, establishing guidelines for effective math and writing journals,
  and attending national conferences on implementing standards

► Providing subs so that grade level teachers can meet at least
  three half days to work on standards implementation plans,
  with minutes reported back to principal

► 100% of staff trained in Standards-Based Learning System, followed up with assistance from Central Support staff Gary
  Cranston, and monthly meetings

► Principal will incorporate standards progression and implementation with each staff member during the evaluation process

- ▶ Reworking teacher prep schedule to provide more common grade level meeting time for teachers

- ▶ Revision and reworking of Academic Achievement Plan to integrate and implement standards in all areas, to be accomplished by five strategic goal teams; every staff member is required to be an active member of a goal team; monthly meetings or as needed; minutes submitted to principal and other staff

- ▶ Technology support of standards in area of oral communication (i.e., hyperstudio projects) and publishing of writing, especially for spring Festival of the Arts

- ▶ Add half-time educational specialist to work with students above standard; set participation criteria using standards in state assessment and classroom

- ▶ Continue to align private and Weighted Student Formula budget to meet needs of EVERY student in getting them to standard and above; each grade level has specifically defined strategies as defined in the Academic Achievement Plan

Community Implementation and Involvement

- ▶ Attend and present at fall Community Forum

- ▶ Publish news articles regarding standards implementation in neighborhood newspaper

- ▶ Student recruitment to include emphasis upon standards and assessments shared in January and February community visits

- ▶ Participate in events such as Rotary Principal for a Day and host other visitors to share the John Hay Standards Story

For Example: Self-Evaluation of Goals 2000 Consortium

Readers of *Getting Excited About Data* will remember a consortium of school districts that began to work collaboratively and strengthen their school improvement efforts and uses of data. Some districts were starting from scratch. Others had several years of training and work with a variety of models and processes. Each model had its own terminology, so it was dangerously easy to slip into arguments over semantics. The group developed Figure 6.2 to outline the seven components of their school improvement blueprint and provide a common vocabulary for discussion.

Four implementation indicators were provided for each of the seven components. The self-evaluation rubric was then used as a diagnostic tool, with each school marking the boxes that described their present status. It also served as a planning tool because it illustrated what the next steps should look like. The same rubric was marked each year to show the progress that had been made toward the "4" column. This demonstrated progress was part of the evidence that the consortium provided in its successful applications for continued funding.

(text continues on page 102)

FIGURE 6.2. G21 Blueprint Self-Evaluation, 1997-1998

G21 Blueprint Self-Evaluation
1997-1998

	1	2	3	4
Structure	Consortium contact-District coordination group	#1 + School level leadership teams (team in each building coordinating with district team); building level planning	#2 + Community component, formation of subcommittees for implementation	School leadership team is active and linked to district team; teacher involvement crosses grades and department lines
Profile	Awareness of use of profile at building level	Profile designed and data collected at building level	Data analyzed at building level with staff involvement	Data applied in goal setting and decision making
Mission	School mission statements exist but are not in alignment with the district mission statement	School mission statements are in alignment with district mission statement and/or beliefs but do not include full participation of shareholders	School mission statements are in alignment with district mission and/or beliefs and were developed with full participation of shareholders	School mission statements are in alignment, developed by shareholders, and provide the direction and focus for decision making
Standards	Shareholders are aware of the concept of standards	Content performance standards are identified (math, language arts, social studies, science)	Curriculum and assessment are aligned with standards	Classroom instructional planning and assessment are standards-referenced

Goals	Target goals are identified by school leadership teams	Working draft of goals developed through staff involvement supported by baseline data	Goals are measurable, performance based, data based, selected by full staff participation, and focused on student learning	Goals are measurable, performance based, data based, selected by full staff participation, focused on student learning, used to focus and consolidate resources and efforts; results drive the improvement plan
Plans	No comprehensive school improvement plan in place	Some elements in place; not clearly evident that there is a connection to student learning	All or most elements evidenced; site-based involvement; clear connection to student learning; staff development plans well developed	Strategies, timelines, and indicators of progress; strong evidence driven by profile; strong site-based involvement; clearly defined staff development activities; goals and timelines specific, feasible, and occurring
Monitoring and Reporting	School complies only with mandates (e.g., WSAS)	Indicators are identified to monitor progress on each school improvement goal	Staff are engaged in regular review of progress indicators in the school improvement plan (internal)	Procedures for both internal and external reviews of progress are in place

Is Our Plan Working?

Figure 5.9 outlined the middle school team's plan for a mentor program. A collection of criteria, parent permissions, training plans, and minutes would provide the indicators that the plan is being implemented. But the goal was to improve student attendance and achievement, so reporting the work done by the adults is not sufficient to answer the question of "How will we know we are getting there?" The success of the plan is determined by whether it has the desired impact on the students—in this case, whether students are in school more, and whether being in school more is contributing to better performance.

In the "where are we now" phase of school improvement, data were gathered on student achievement to assess the current situation. The same data should be compiled annually to develop a longitudinal look at progress and can be portrayed in run charts.

When schools worked to identify "where we want to go," part of the effort was to take the major components of mission and belief statements and make them concrete with observable indicators. Chapter 4 provided the example of a school that wanted its students to become lifelong learners and needed to articulate what a lifelong learner looks like and sounds like at various ages. Gathering information on these indicators would become part of the monitoring stage as the school addressed the "How will we know we are getting there?" question. The tools that were introduced to display data in Chapters 3 and 5 are tools that can be used again and again throughout the process.

Many of us who learned and use Madeline Hunter's synthesis of theory and research related to effective instruction[2] have difficulty saying the word *monitor* without adding *and adjust*. This is true for the implementation phase of school improvement. Although we needed specific action plans to set realistic timelines, acquire needed resources, and avoid overloading ourselves with too many complex efforts, those action plans must be considered "carved in Jell-O." If results cannot be observed, or the changes we see are not the intended, desired ones, school leadership teams must acknowledge and address those facts. They will need to verify whether the action plan is being implemented as intended, and they may have to modify it on the basis of resources, unexpected barriers, and other needs that arise. They may need to reexamine whether the strategies selected for implementation should be changed. School leaders, however, must also use caution and guard against premature decisions to abandon a course before it has had time for a true test. The challenge is to strike a proper balance between flexibility and evolutionary planning on the one hand and patience and perseverance on the other.

Monitoring progress is not always a sophisticated and complicated endeavor. Sometimes principals agree to conduct business on the roof, kiss a pig, or sit in a dunking booth if students read a million pages—and parent volunteers construct a huge paper thermometer to count the pages that have been read. That is a way of monitoring progress that can motivate continued effort until the real results (higher reading scores) can be documented.

For Example: John Bullen Middle School
Evaluation Plan

John Bullen Middle School[3] was a junior high until 3 years ago when it was reconfigured to house grades six through eight. As part of its transformation to a middle school, the staff chose the Accelerated Schools model for school governance and comprehensive school reform design. Their journey of change could be mapped on Figure 2.1.

First, they spent a year and involved a broad range of shareholders in development of a vision and **mission** statement. Then they compiled their **school portfolio** that included academic achievement data from the Iowa Tests of Basic Skills and the Wisconsin Student Assessment System, discipline data, and perceptual data from the Accelerated Schools Process survey. During the summer, the entire staff participated in the "Taking Stock" phase of the Accelerated Schools Process and discussed the data, using the inquiry process.

From the **concerns** that emerged, they identified four **priority goal** areas:

◆ Discipline

◆ Parent involvement

◆ Teaching and learning

◆ Communications

A cadre was formed to **study** each of these goal areas and recommend **strategies**. At this point, I became involved as the external coach and met with each cadre. That first visit was a little messy. People who had volunteered for the discipline cadre were entrenched in two camps, one for improving the new discipline plan and one committed to eliminating it. The parent involvement cadre included parents but had quite different versions of what parent involvement should look like and who owned the problem. Some members of the communications cadre were carrying big axes to grind on the principal and central office. The teaching and learning cadre was the most harmonious group, but two big things were missing. Members weren't clear on their role, and they hadn't spent much time discussing the student performance data that were included in their school portfolio. So they didn't have answers for some of my initial questions:

◆ What specific area of student achievement is your focus?

◆ What is your leadership role in applying the training you've had in Dimensions of Learning?

◆ Where does introduction of the Schoolwide Enrichment Model fit with your overall instructional program and school reform design?

◆ What are the results you want to be able to report as a consequence of these strategies?

Each of these cadres had some problems to work through, but that is not a criticism. I was neither surprised nor disappointed. They were exactly where most groups are when they begin to work together! And they made rapid progress during that year. When I came back the next spring, they had reached agreement on the **strategies** they would recommend to the full staff. The discipline cadre had healed their conflicts and agreed to work on (a) consistent implementation of the Honor Level System and (b) improving the effectiveness of in-school suspension.

The parent involvement cadre had followed through on my recommendation to study Joyce Epstein's research and learn about the Parent Involvement Network through Johns Hopkins University. They had identified an ambitious agenda for (a) Parents in Education nights, (b) Lighted Schoolhouse activities, (c) a more reliable and current Calendar of Events so parents would *know* about the opportunities for involvement, (d) a directory of parents with interests they could share and ways they would like to volunteer, (e) a directory of teachers with their pictures and some personal information to help build connections with parents and students, (f) formation of a Community Action Team to deal with the issues that needed a broader coalition beyond parents, and (g) continuing with the Parent Teacher Student Association.

The teaching and learning cadre had studied the data and uncovered a need to expand the Learning Support Program so more students had access. They had also made the connection between the Powerful Learning component of Accelerated Schools and their plans for application of the Dimensions of Learning and use of the Schoolwide Enrichment Model in sixth grade. A Comprehensive Reform grant of $77,777 from the state of Wisconsin provided resources for a significant group of staff to travel and receive in-depth training in all these designs.

The communications cadre had also prepared recommendations to (a) add a staff issues page to the Thursday bulletin, (b) identify staff liaisons and form a mediation team, (c) expand parent-teacher communication through technology such as classroom telephones and e-mail, and (d) include team-building activities in professional development plans.

Now they were ready for coaching on the **action plans** that would be needed. They were surprised at the dogged way we had to keep slugging through nuts-and-bolts questions such as these:

◆ And what would need to happen before that?
◆ How could you arrange time for that to happen?
◆ Then what could you *stop* doing with that time?
◆ Have you transferred all the steps you promised in your grant applications into these plans so your efforts are consolidated?

They were cooperative and worked hard because they realized that they had to sell their recommendations to the rest of the staff. They knew that it would be hard to build strong commitment if they weren't ready with some preliminary answers to the "if we agree, how would it work" questions, so they really buckled down and hammered it out. They also said it was the hardest part of the process because "we like to procrastinate and leave the details for later." The words used here—*dogged, slugging, buckled,* and *hammered*—were their words as each cadre worked for half a day on their action plans and developed the main points for their presentation to staff. I left again, they went to their staff, and all the recommendations were accepted.

My next trip to Bullen focused on the **indicators** they would use in the Evaluation Plan they needed for their Comprehensive School Reform Design grant. I spent another half day with each cadre. We reviewed the applications they had written for every grant so we could be sure that every type of evidence that would be needed was included and would be gathered along the way. We didn't want to lose any possibilities of continued funding. Nor did we want to have people scrambling for documentation at the last minute before filing the next application.

We also didn't want to pile on a lot of extra work to meet evaluation requirements, so we started by referring back to all the types of data they had at their disposal already. Figure 6.3 is the grid we constructed to represent their comprehensive evaluation plan, based on the "monitoring and evaluation" column of all the action plans. As noted at the bottom, it includes both qualitative and quantitative evidence.

FIGURE 6.3. Cadre Evaluation Tools

Cadre Evaluation Tools

Tools	Attendance, Sign-in Sheets	Flyers, notices, articles	Meeting notes, documents	Assignment sheets in ISS	Staff Survey	Parent Survey	Student Survey/Intervie	Targeted Methodology	Overall GPA Analysis	Overall Test Score Analysis	% participation in Extra-curricular Activities
Discipline											
Consistent implementation of HLS	X		X					Analysis of infractions by category			
Improving effectiveness of ISS				X				Improvement of grades and decrease of use by ISS users			
Parent Involvement											
P.I.E nights	X	X						Parents come; grades up and homework up	X	X	
Lighted schoolhouse	X	X					X				
Calendar of events		X					X			X	
Directory of parents to volunteer			Directory X		X	X					
Directory of teachers' pictures and information			Directory X		X	X					
Community action team	To be developed in the future										
Continue PTSA	To be developed in the future										
Teaching and Learning											
Powerful Learning											
Application of Dimension of Learning			Training participation X		X					Analysis by level	
School-wide Enrichment Model							X	Analysis by Friday attendance			
Expanded Learning Support			House plans X		X		X	Pre- and post-test		Analysis by level	
Communications											
Thursday bulletin with staff issues page			X		X						
Staff liaisons, mediation team	X		X		X			# of referrals and resolutions			
Technology for better parent-teacher communications					X	X		Homework completion			
E-mail; dismantle computer lab			X		X						
Team-building activities	X				X						
	Qualitative Measures							**Quantitative Measures**			

One column has the heading "Targeted Methodology." This is where we reported specific types of data collection or analysis that would be needed to demonstrate the results of particular interventions and accomplishment of related goals. Every other notation or *X* on this grid represents evidence already available that could be gathered throughout the year, ready to attach and send away with grant reports and new applications—and also ready to publicize and celebrate at home.

Are We Fulfilling Our Mission?

Chapter 5 addressed the question "How will we get there?" and underscored the importance of planning our work so that it matches our mission, can accomplish our goals, and can produce the results we described when we answered the question of "Where do we want to go?" This chapter has explained and provided examples of indicators that tell us if we're implementing the plan and if it's having the impact we intended. We also need to consciously check our plan for congruence with our mission statement. Do we have evidence that the strategies we chose are consistent with our values and that the data we collect will reflect the outcomes we really want?

Back in Chapter 4, we encountered a school with a passion for lifelong learning. They brainstormed the characteristics of a lifelong learner that they would be able to see developing within their own students, even at an early age. They included things such as "gets interested in something," "goes to the library (or Internet) to learn more about it," "starts projects on his own," "tries to get other people interested," and "likes to figure out her own way to do it." But what if the instructional program is so prescriptive that a student doesn't have the chance to get interested in something on her own? What if trying to get someone else interested in your topic is considered cheating? What if figuring out your own way to do it doesn't match any of the boxes on the rubric? We need to be careful what we put in our mission statement—because then we have to demonstrate what we're doing to fulfill it *and* be sure we're not doing things that actually prevent it.

Another school faced a similar challenge from their mission statement that included the phrase "prepared to live in a democratic, pluralistic society." It sounded great. But the staff was concerned about the reality of the rhetoric. The student population was quite homogeneous racially and economically, and staff members wondered if students were really aware of issues and needs outside their own environment. The observable behaviors that they decided to monitor were participation in student government, increased roles for students in shared decision making, active participation in that year's county and state elections, and participation in community service projects. Students in civics classes became involved in identifying opportunities for student involvement, and students in math classes gathered the data on participation rates to show results. These school leaders realized that the existing culture of their school did not empower students to get practice doing the very things they wanted them to do as adults, so they had to alter some of their own roles and create new opportunities.

For Example: Block Scheduling

One of the most frequent high school reforms of this decade has been the trend toward block scheduling. Advocates say that these longer periods have both academic and affective benefits. On the academic side, they claim that deeper learning can occur through more in-depth exploration of a topic. On the affective side, teachers and students can get to know each other better because they encounter fewer different individuals each day.

It sounds logical to me, and I'm a believer in larger blocks of time. One of the reasons I started out in elementary, rather than secondary, education was the usual reason—I love little kids. But the other reason I didn't want to teach high school was an aspect I hated when I was in high school myself. I had some *wonderful* high school teachers, but just when Mr. Engberg got a really great debate going about the central issue in a piece of classical literature, the bell would ring. And just when I got really rolling on an essay, the bell would ring. And just when I was about to nail my geometry teacher or physics teacher with "but *why* does it work this way?" they'd get "saved" by the bell.

So I support block scheduling, but I still want to know about data, evidence, indicators, and results. I ask people with block schedules if they're working—and they say yes. Then I ask them how they know. So far, they haven't been telling me about how they are documenting the evidence they have that kids *are* learning at higher levels. They haven't described the indicators they have that students and teachers know each other better or that students report feeling safer, more secure, more nurtured, and so forth. The only "data-based" answer I've received to date has been, "The number of discipline referrals for disruptive behavior in the halls has dropped in half." (Well, if they're in the halls only half as often as they used to be, what would you expect?)

The indicators we choose to monitor as evidence of implementation and impact tell a lot about what we really value. Is it less disruption we value, or more powerful learning? When we answer the question "How will we know we are getting there?" we must be sure our mission is alive and well—not missing in action.

For Example: Nathan Hale High School

Remember the panel discussion at the high school reform seminar in Chapter 5? One of the speakers described the principle of personalization and then reported the change to an eight-period day, and people had trouble seeing the connection. Contrast that example with the perseverance to move from general principles and ideals to congruent, concrete reality that is exemplified by the careful planning and conscientious monitoring at Nathan Hale High School.[4]

This school of 1,080 students reflects the diversity of urban Seattle and serves a large population of special education and English as a Second Language students. In 1994, a core group of teacher leaders began to explore the Common Principles of the Coalition of Essential Schools (CES), but formal membership in CES did not occur until 1997. These years of cautious exploration and collegial dialogue paid off in dramatic change in just 4 years' time.

Hale now uses a modified block schedule, has created a schoolwide mentorship program, requires junior and senior projects and community service for graduation, and makes "personalization of education" its greatest strength and most effective selling point with students and parents.

The personalization occurs through creation of heterogeneously balanced ninth-grade academies, begun in the fall of 1998. Each academy houses 125 ninth graders, staffed by six teachers, realizing a student-to-teacher ratio of approximately 20:1. Students earn science, health, language arts, and social studies credit. Academic and behavioral standards apply to all students, and honors work can be arranged through separate contracts.

Teachers collaborate during common prep time to encourage consistent policies and practices, flexible scheduling, strong communication links, and focused use of mentorships. Professional development focuses on examining student and teacher work through five Critical Friends groups involving more than 85% of the staff.

The 10th-grade Integrated Studies Program began the following year as students moved upward. The Futures Committee is currently developing advanced placement/specialty classes and expanding job shadowing and internship programs for 11th and 12th graders to continue the personalized approach.

The ability to forge schoolwide commitment around a set of principles and then define them in concrete terms and implement them is exceptional in itself. But as Principal Eric Benson points out, the purpose was to improve high school life for students, and it has. Compared with ninth-grade statistics before the academies were implemented, Hale's freshman attendance has increased from 84% to 92%, the average grade point average has grown from 2.55 to 2.78, the dropout rate has dropped from 6% to 2%, and discipline problems have plummeted from 29% to 1%. Grades 9, 10, and 11 have all demonstrated gains on the norm-referenced standardized tests given in the district.

The intended payoff for students has brought benefits to the school as a whole. Nathan Hale High School has received more than $225,000 in grants to fund educational tools and personnel, including a 1998 National Endowment for the Humanities Planning Grant and a 1998-2001 Washington State Inclusion Grant. In a district in which parents and students can choose any of 10 high schools, Nathan Hale was rated No. 1 on district parent/staff surveys and No. 2 on student surveys.

Notes

1. John Hay Elementary School can be reached at 201 Garfield Street, Seattle, WA 98109, telephone 206-378-2710, or by e-mailing Principal Joanne Testacross (jtesta@johnhay.ssd.k12.wa.us).

2. As I read the new books and attend workshops on brain research, I keep wondering, *Does anybody else out there see the match with her descriptions of elements of motivation and meaning and correct level of difficulty and active participation and more?* If the only thing you associate with the name Madeline Hunter is a seven-step lesson plan checklist, please know—that was not her work, and it does not do justice to one of the century's most thorough, conscientious efforts to build a bridge between theory and research, and the realities of the classroom.

3. For an update on school transformation at John Bullen Middle School, contact Principal Blane McCann, or teacher leaders Jim Fergus and Terri Huck at 262-597-4460 (e-mail addresses are bmccann@kusd.edu, jfergus@kusd.edu, and thuck@kusd.edu).

4. To learn more about the best practices exemplified at Nathan Hale High School, call Principal Eric Benson at 206-366-7800 or e-mail Janet Blanford (jbarks@hale.ssd.k12.wa.us), Ed Hopfner (ehopfner@hale.ssd.k12.wa.us), Sarah Smith (ssmith@hale.ssd.k12.wa.us), or Gia Truong (gtruong@hale.ssd.k12.wa.us).

7

Answering the "How Will We Sustain the Focus and Momentum?" Question

While writing the first edition, I watched the city of Baltimore honor a hero. Cal Ripken Jr. had broken Lou Gehrig's record of playing in 2,130 consecutive games. The numerals on the warehouse across from the diamond flipped to 2,131, and the crowd went wild. Cal just smiled and loped around the field as if he wasn't too sure what the fuss was all about. How did he reach that milestone? He just kept showing up for work. Along the way, he struck out at the plate now and then and recorded some errors in his position as shortstop. But he just kept showing up for work and doing his best. He knew how to sustain focus and momentum.[1]

How can travelers on the road to school improvement develop that same tenacity? How do school leaders add momentum to the *M* of maintenance in RPTIM (Figure 1.1)? How does the innovation that was implemented in response to "How will we get there?" become institutionalized so that it is taken for granted as "just the way we do things around here"? Quality improvement users would say that you do so by repeating the PDCA cycle—now that you've checked what you've done, act on the information, and start again with planning. Those steps are important, but inadequate. They overestimate the power of technical processes and underestimate the power of the prevailing school culture. The scientific law that an object at rest tends to remain at rest is nowhere more true than in traditional organizations. Great leaders and great ideas have sparked new efforts that blaze briefly and sputter into oblivion because they are smothered under the overwhelming weight of the school culture. Lasting change requires reculturing, reshaping the norms of the organization—what the gurus of the early 1990s called *paradigm shifting*. This chapter describes six actions that are needed to sustain change:

◆ Understand and respond to reactions

◆ Continue training and coaching

◆ Cope with conflict

◆ Build a culture of inquiry

◆ Refocus and reaffirm organizational values

◆ Support leaders and followers

Understand and Respond to Reactions

Organizations are made up of human beings with vast prior experience and a wide range of personal needs and interests. To sustain a change effort, we must know how to recognize these needs and respond appropriately.

Children learn in different ways and at different speeds. In much the same way, adults adjust to change in different ways and at different rates. The concerns-based adoption model (CBAM) is based on studies of how teachers react to new innovations. One component of the model identifies a developmental sequence of stages of concern through which people move as they accept and adjust to change. *Taking Charge of Change*, published by the Association for Supervision and Curriculum Development, describes the progression of concerns:

◆ Awareness

◆ Information

◆ Personal

◆ Management

◆ Consequence

◆ Collaboration

◆ Refocusing

Once individuals in the organization become aware of an impending or a developing change, their first concerns revolve around wanting to know more about it and how they will be affected personally. As their questions are answered and they become willing to attempt the new practice, their concerns relate to how they will manage logistics such as time, materials, and record keeping. When these concerns of self and the task are addressed, teachers become more interested in how their use of a new practice is affecting students. More advanced stages of concern relate to sharing their new efforts with colleagues and using their own ideas to modify and improve the new practice. As part of CBAM, the researchers developed procedures for assessing the concerns of individuals within the organization.

Stages of Concern Questionnaire

The Stages of Concern Questionnaire (SoCQ) is a survey instrument that includes 35 items and requires only 10 to 15 minutes to administer. It can be hand or machine scored. The result is a profile that shows the intensity of each concern for that respondent. Average scores of groups or subgroups can be calculated.

Purpose. The SoCQ and the variations described below are designed to identify the most intense concerns felt by individuals and groups in the organization. This information is valuable in planning organizational responses and support for its members.

When to Use. The formal SoCQ procedure is generally used when research or program evaluation is being conducted. It can also be used to provide diagnostic information during a change process. It can be administered several times during a year without losing its reliability.

Whom to Involve. The SoCQ can be used with an entire school or district population in its machine-scorable form.

Materials Needed. The survey items and quick-scoring device are included in *Taking Charge of Change.* Respondents will need the survey form and pencils. For large groups, answer sheets that can be scanned and analyzed should be used.

Tips for Facilitators

The SoCQ itself is easy to administer, and the profiles produced from the results appear deceptively self-evident. The challenge is to interpret them accurately and respond appropriately. Study the descriptions in *Taking Charge of Change* carefully. If the SoCQ is to be used for formal program evaluation, the SoCQ manual and training in interpretation of SoCQ profiles should be acquired.

For Example: Cooperative Learning

In the Winter 1995 issue of the *Journal of Staff Development,* Stephen Anderson, Carol Rolheiser, and Barrie Bennett reported their use of the SoCQ to document the experiences of teachers who were implementing cooperative learning. They discovered that the teachers surveyed seemed to cluster into three groups, which they called nonusers, tentative beginning users, and experienced beginning users. They identified nine concerns that were common to all three groups, although the concerns varied in intensity from group to group:

- ◆ Impact on teaching strategies

- ◆ Curriculum integration

- ◆ Time for implementation

- ◆ Student participation

- ◆ Individualization

- ◆ Student assessment and evaluation

- ◆ Student outcomes

- ◆ Collaboration with other teachers

- ◆ Quality of implementation

Because these concerns were felt by all participants, the authors were able to suggest alterations in the schools' staff development programs that would respond and provide support for growth to the next stage.

A Variation: One-Legged Interviews

The SoCQ is the most formal method of identifying the concerns felt by participants in a change process. *Taking Charge of Change* also describes the use of face-to-face conversations in which the facilitator asks simple questions such as "How do you feel about ————?" and may follow up with more specific probes. This informal dialogue has been referred to as a "one-legged interview" because it should be concise enough to be completed before the facilitator would lose her balance if she were on one leg. To interpret the responses correctly, the facilitator must not interrupt and then must reflect on the entire conversation and analyze it holistically to assess the stage of concern being expressed.

Another Twist: Feedback Form

The authors of *Taking Charge of Change* also describe the use of an open-ended statement such as "When you think about ————, what are your concerns?" Their recommendations are to regard this as more formal than the face-to-face conversation, encouraging respondents to answer in complete sentences. They also suggest two forms of analysis, first considering each sentence separately and then rereading and analyzing the tone of the whole response.

To use the open-ended statement for program evaluation or research, facilitators should read the authors' recommendations carefully and be thorough in their interpretation. I have found that even an informal open-ended statement can provide valuable information for purposes of "quick and dirty" diagnosis and adjustments to staff development activities. I include an item such as "My biggest concern about ———— at this time is ————" on feedback forms at the end of training sessions. Although the interpretation can hardly be called scientific, I review the feedback forms with stages of concern in mind, which helps me make adjustments in follow-up sessions. It also indicates whether participants share common concerns or have a wide range of needs that will require a greater variety of responses.

Continue Training and Coaching

A difficulty with every school improvement project I have encountered is that the schools spend too large a proportion of their professional development resources on training before implementing a new innovation. The implication is that we can "front-end load" a process that takes years and requires individual movement through several stages of acceptance and use. The assumption is that adult learners can acquire new skills all at once, in isolation from practice, and can retain and retrieve them for use once the system has removed barriers and set them free to proceed. Conducting all the training at the beginning further ignores the reality that through the years, there may be considerable staff turnover. New people join the organization who were never introduced to techniques they will be expected to use. The quality management concept of "just in time" training is not a panacea but does respond to the adult learners' need for job relevancy and immediate application of the new learning.

Continued training should be of two types. Introductory or basic training should be repeated on a cyclical basis to include new staff members and those who may have attended earlier training but have not yet had a chance to implement it. For instructional approaches as complex as cooperative learning, interdisciplinary teaching, or learning styles, a sequence from basic to more advanced training experiences should be provided. These levels of training can respond to the needs of participants as they move through the stages of concern. Knowing that a higher level of training is available can also stimulate the progress of more cautious adopters.

Coaching is different from training and resembles the guided practice stage of instruction. Feedback is needed for those who are most active with the new technique, as well as those who are least skilled. The leaders need to refine and polish their practice because they are models for others and need to be sure they are providing accurate examples. Those least skilled, or most reluctant, need coaching to convey the expectation that they will continue to improve their art and craft in line with organizational goals.

For Example: External Coach

I am currently involved in three types of coaching, all of which are important to continued success in a change effort. Later in this section, I'll describe coaching as providing feedback to principals. In another section, I'll talk about being a coach of support specialists who, in turn, coach teachers.

The most intense of the three coaching roles is that of external coach, which I described in the Chapter 6 story about John Bullen Middle School. This type of "critical friend" visits a school on a regular basis to review progress and feedback, present some "next steps" training or review and refresh previous training, and guide the actual work of application. One of the teacher leaders at John Bullen Middle School wrote to me about my role there:

> You have shown us that you like and respect us. You have spent a lot of time with us carefully listening and probing with questions such as "Do I hear you saying that . . . ?" Second, you have a done a great job of staying objective. After listening and clarifying, you put our thoughts into some sort of graphic format that we have all agreed on and can use to stay on track in future.

This coaching role is quite different from training and from consulting.

A trainer engages learners in acquisition of new knowledge and skills and may provide suggestions for follow-up activities, but a trainer leaves. A consultant studies a situation and makes recommendations on how to solve problems or take appropriate action. The organization can choose whether to implement the suggestions. The consulting role is more customized and focused than training, but a consultant also leaves. A coach, on the other hand, is right there on the sidelines during the game, helping design the plays, giving the halftime pep talks, and enjoying the applause or enduring the loss along with the team.

A Variation:
Academic Achievement Plan Review

Another role of a coach is to provide feedback. As a central office staff (not line) administrator, my role with principals is one of coaching and support. For several years, principals have been expected to work with their school leadership teams and develop documents called strategic plans, school improvement plans, and now academic achievement plans. As mentioned in Chapter 3, their planning process includes developing the site-based budget, staffing package, and professional development plan. Their plans had in previous years been turned in to their supervisors, and copies were made for the people in budget, human resources, special education, and compensatory education who were to verify that all compliance requirements had been met. But principals heard nothing in return unless some major issue was caught in the compliance review.

This year was different. All the principals were asked to come (with members of their leadership team if possible) and present their academic achievement plans to a panel that included the school supervisor and the others who had been nameless faces checking compliance in past years. Presenters were asked to talk about the collaborative process that was used to develop their plan, the data they reviewed and how the data guided their work, how their chosen strategies matched the needs of special populations, and so on. Through the dialogue, central office administrators gained a greater appreciation of school efforts, and school leaders received affirmation, immediate feedback, coaching on anything that needed to be revised, and suggestions for future consideration.

I asked several principals what they thought of this new process, and their answers were almost identical. "It was nerve-racking to anticipate, and kind of intimidating until I started talking, but then it was really fun to have a listening audience that cared about my school and would understand what we're trying to do. And it was so much better than having our plans disappear into the black hole at A & S" (the Administration and Support Center).

Another Twist: Mike Holmgren

One of my favorite coaches in the world of sports is Mike Holmgren. I got curious about him when he was the quarterback coach in San Francisco, and my football hero was Joe Montana. I started focusing on Holmgren himself when I was a Wisconsinite, watching him smooth the rough edges off a Mississippi kid named Bret Favre and build the Green Bay Packers into Super Bowl champions. I was thrilled when he decided to come to Seattle a few months after I did—and occasionally claimed credit for his move. Maybe I find Mike fascinating because he was a high school history teacher—and now that he puts on reading glasses along with his headset and clipboard, he really fits the image. My point in this example is that a coach is a teacher who gives feedback on performance and keeps track of whether the learning occurs.

One year, Joey Galloway was a holdout, came back late in the season, wasn't very effective, and then left for the Dallas Cowboys. There weren't many broken hearts in Seattle. Most of the people interviewed on the street expressed a sentiment of "good riddance." But when I heard Coach Holmgren speak at our

Seahawks Academy for middle school students who need a chance to turn around their lives, he was apologizing for having failed in that situation. People at the tables near me were saying, "Who cares?" or "Why should he feel bad about that?" But Coach Holmgren said, "My job has always been about building up people. If I lose somebody, I take it personally, whether it's a ninth grader, a high school senior, or a player." Coaching in the arena of school change is all about keeping people in the game.

Cope With Conflict

It is in the nature of humans to differ, and from those differences conflicts are bound to arise. One of the most popular topics for consultants in the 1990s was conflict resolution. Unfortunately, the term *resolution* implies an unrealistic expectation that conflict can be eliminated and that the presence of conflict is a bad thing. I prefer to talk about managing conflict or coping with conflict because this acknowledges that a certain amount is unavoidable and that productive organizations often encourage it. Dynamic organizations are not populated by clones. "Groupthink" is a powerful killer of creativity. I have successfully used four techniques to cope with conflict: Venn diagrams, Quick-Writes, TalkWalks, and Go for the Green.

Venn Diagrams

A Venn diagram is simply a set of two or more circles. They are drawn to intersect, be concentric, or not touch at all as a way of illustrating relationships. The name comes from the originator, mathematician John Venn, who specialized in logic.

Purpose. A Venn diagram can be used to illustrate complex relationships, display data, or generate discussion for problem solving and decision making. Venn diagrams help groups compare and contrast multiple sets of ideas or interests and are particularly valuable for demonstrating relationships that are difficult to describe in words.

When to Use. When members of a group are polarized and lack a sense of common ground, a Venn diagram can reopen communication and refocus the group.

Whom to Involve. All members of the group, or parties to a conflict, should contribute to the Venn diagram.

Materials Needed. Paper and pencil are sufficient. Chart paper and stick-on notes are useful for constructing Venn diagrams that can be seen and discussed by larger groups.

Tips for Facilitators

Describe the purpose of a Venn diagram and present a simple example. Engage the group in determining how many circles will be needed and predicting

FIGURE 7.1. Venn Diagram of Topics for Character Education

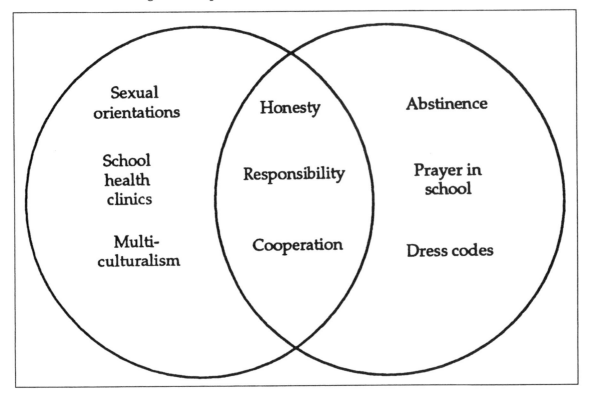

how much they will overlap. Give instructions about writing their responses, one on each stick-on note. Small groups may sketch their own Venn diagram to share, or a large diagram can be developed as participants post their stick-on notes. Be flexible and add or move circles as the group's responses are compiled.

For Example: Character Education

To answer the "Where do we want to go?" question, a Venn diagram can be used to discover the common values and beliefs held by various shareholder groups. Each group (parents, teachers, community members, students) can meet separately and write its beliefs or interests, one per stick-on note. A large Venn diagram can be drawn with a circle representing each of the groups. The stick-on notes can then be placed in separate or overlapping areas of the circles. This communicates visually which values are shared by which groups. If even a few stick-on notes land in the centermost overlapping area, the group can see that there are shared values on which to build.

In many districts, the public is calling for renewed emphasis on character education but have diverse agendas as to what should be included. Some school leaders have courageously brought conflicting groups together to seek common ground. Figure 7.1 is a Venn diagram that illustrates the consensus reached.

Variations

Venn diagrams can be used during almost any phase of an improvement process. To answer the "Where are we now?" question, a group could use the circles to represent major forces or entities in the organization and how they are related or influence each other.

Quick-Writes

A Quick-Write is similar to the informal stream-of-consciousness writing that is done in keeping a journal or log. A prompt is given, and participants are encouraged to record their thoughts as they emerge.

Purpose. The Quick-Write provides an opportunity for individual, reflective thinking about the topic or issue at hand.

When to Use. The Quick-Write can be used before initiating discussion about a complex or controversial issue. In this case, the purpose is to help participants clarify their own viewpoints and prepare words with which to express themselves before launching into position statements. The Quick-Write is also helpful as a tension reliever if a serious discussion is deadlocked or is becoming too inflammatory. Participants are asked to take a silent break and put their current position or issues into writing. This guides them to refocus and then reopen the discussion on a more positive note.

Whom to Involve. When Quick-Write is used to open discussion or deal with conflicts, all parties should be involved.

Materials Needed. Individual paper and writing instruments should be supplied. Markers and chart paper should not be in evidence because Quick-Write participants are promised confidentiality.

Tips for Facilitators

Provide a writing prompt in the form of a sentence stem or heading. Assure participants that they are writing to clarify their own thoughts and decide how they can best express those thoughts to others. Their writing remains their own property, and they share only what they decide to after they have completed the activity.

For Example: Who Should Be in Charge?

The district's site-based management advisory committee was meeting in an attempt to create better understanding between principals and representatives from some schools who felt that they were not being given enough authority in enough areas of school operation. Some of the parents and community members had complained to board members that principals were "holding out" and trying to retain control. Principals were upset and feeling threatened. Among themselves and to a few district administrators, they whispered that the district was "giving the ship away" and that it seemed unfair for them to be held accountable for their schools' success when the decisions were being taken out of their hands.

As an outside facilitator, I began the meeting by asking participants to do some writing on a form I had prepared. The blue sheets that I gave to principals had these headings:

I became a principal   Even though I knew
because I wanted to: I would have to:

The green sheets given to parent and community representatives were headed:

I want to be part of   But not deal with
these decisions: these decisions:

When the participants had received their sheets, I asked them how much work time they would need, and I emphasized that they would be working independently. A time limit of 5 minutes was set, and they began to write.

When the time was up, I asked them to form groups with two or three blue sheets and two or three green sheets in evidence. Their instructions were to share their thoughts with each other. They could simply place their sheets on the table next to each other and make comparisons or set their sheets aside and just express the overall feelings that emerged as they reflected on their roles in shared decision making.

Some groups looked at each other warily, and communication was slow to start. Other groups were able to candidly compare their feelings. They discovered that principals had worked hard to achieve administrative roles because they wanted to be instructional leaders. They wanted to work with teachers to improve instruction and wanted to be advocates for children. These were their primary motivators, despite their knowledge that they would have to deal with personnel issues, budget management, and paperwork for the organization. Parent and community members had indicated that they wanted to talk about what should be in the curriculum and how teachers should teach—maybe even evaluate teachers—but not be involved in firing them or in dealing with any element of "the bureaucracy." As they talked, the site-based management team members began to realize that they had been pushing to take over all the things that principals had seen as their real purpose and leave principals with only those tasks that were "the drudgery." Some principals began quietly to share how it felt to work for years trying to develop leadership skills and feel reduced to being a manager of the noneducational aspects of the school. This open discussion was the first step toward defining the roles of shareholder groups and clarifying the scope of site-based management for the district.

TalkWalks

TalkWalking is a technique I learned from my friend Pam Robbins, who developed it in collaboration with a physician friend. It is based on the practice of "going on rounds" with students and colleagues in a teaching hospital. It adds the kinesthetic learning modality that is too often missing from the typical "sit and get" staff development workshop.

Purpose. Going on a TalkWalk provides an opportunity for colleagues to exchange viewpoints in an informal atmosphere. It combines interaction with the stimulation of exercise and a change of scenery. The movement and change of environment are helpful in overcoming inhibitions and promoting a sense of well-being.

When to Use. A TalkWalk can be helpful on many occasions. It can be used toward the end of a workshop to allow participants to discuss the implications of what they have learned and how they can apply it in their job role. It can also become an informal part of the school culture. Staff members can choose times to meet for both mental and physical exercise, combining a brisk walk with discussion of an article they have read or an idea they would like to try. Colleagues can use a TalkWalk to seek each other's advice on a challenge they are currently facing. As a tool for coping with conflict, a TalkWalk can provide a chance to ease a group out of a tense situation or nonproductive discussion by breaking participants up into smaller groups and moving them into another setting.

Whom to Involve. Any group of two or three persons can engage in a TalkWalk. In addition to workshop participants, variations have included teachers and students, or principal and teacher(s). One friend of mine declares that a TalkWalk is the only way she's ever found to get her teenage son to open up and communicate with her.

Materials Needed. The ideal environment for TalkWalking is a place where participants can get outdoors and walk around the block or parking lot. TalkWalking has also been effective in the confines of hotel corridors and conference centers. The main requirement is space to move out and away from the confines of the existing situation—both mentally and physically.

Tips for Facilitators

Set a time limit and a topic. Create a definite expectation that this is not just an extra break but a task-oriented activity. State the purpose clearly, such as "Come back with your analysis of why we are having difficulty with this topic and your recommendation of where we should go from here."

Use your own discretion about forming the dyads or trios for TalkWalking. On some occasions, I have orchestrated the structure to get particular participants or groups talking to each other or to break up certain combinations that were sidetracking the whole group. Unless there is a specific reason for directing the structure of the groups, voluntary choices of partners are best.

For Example: Unsuspecting Recruits

It was a long, hot summer. I was one of several consultants hired to provide training for school leadership teams who would face new responsibilities under recent state legislation. Two weeklong institutes had already been held with good results. The in-state facilitators who were working with me had done a great job, the content was well received, and the groups had left with the first draft of a school improvement plan in hand so they could complete it at their schools and submit it to the state in a timely manner. This Monday morning was totally unlike the others. When the state facilitators and I arrived, the people at the host school were friendly but had no knowledge about the supplies and materials we were expecting. Coffeepots had been packed away for the summer, and their whereabouts were unknown—always a bad sign. The participants arrived and were polite, but they seemed distant and wary. As I began the overview of the week and talked about the final product we would create by Friday, they became more tense. The body language became rigid and hostile, and it was almost impossible to establish eye contact.

After struggling for nearly an hour, I decided to stop talking and introduce a short videotape. While I "huddled" with my copresenters to analyze the situation, I watched the participants pass written notes and exchange nonverbal messages that seemed less than positive. My colleagues couldn't shed any light on what was happening, so I decided to take a risk and confront the situation. It didn't seem as if I had a lot to lose, because I'd never had them with me anyway.

When the videotape was over, I told them that I'd like to give them a chance to discuss the ideas in it but that I also needed their help. I described the feeling I had that we were not quite on the same wavelength and that I'd appreciate their suggestions on what might be done to create a better climate. I then described a TalkWalk and asked them to come back in 10 minutes. By then, coffee would be ready, and we would take a 15-minute break (emphasizing that the walk was an activity, not a break). I asked them to either have the bravest member of their group talk to me during the break or give me an anonymous written note of feedback.

I wasn't sure how to interpret the enthusiasm with which they accepted the opportunity to get together and move out, but they did accept the assignment. The feedback I received was invaluable. They had been shocked at my opening comments that they were members of leadership teams and that we would be working together on improvement plans for their school. Many of them had been contacted just the week before and had been asked to attend a 5-day workshop. They were going to receive a stipend for attending, with an option of graduate credit, and the only prerequisite they knew about was that they were available. I asked them to set aside their confusion about their roles and learn what they could that day about the research on effective schools while I sought clarification of their responsibilities.

That evening was spent on the telephone. Many calls flew back and forth to and from staff members at the state education department, local district administrators, my copresenters, and me. We asked administrators from each district to come the next morning and meet with their participants to clarify the purpose of the workshop and their responsibilities that week and in follow-up with their schools. To their credit, every district cooperated, and the first part of Tuesday morning was spent in breakout rooms laying the groundwork that should have been in place earlier. Some people dropped out and left. Those who stayed became one of the most cooperative groups I've worked with, eager to learn and fulfill their roles.

That TalkWalk provided the tension release they needed and the information I needed with which to make changes in our relationship and purpose. I hate to speculate on what would have happened without it.

Go for the Green

Bob Garmston introduced this activity at a workshop called Premier Presentation Skills, which I attended several years ago. It is one of the most valuable techniques I have found to address conflicts and nonproductive behavior in groups.

Purpose. Go for the Green appeals to the senses through its use of color and metaphor. The purpose is to identify possible causes for nonproductive behavior and shift the focus from the problem behavior or the problem people to factors that can be changed more readily.

When to Use. Go for the Green can be used when groups, or the facilitators of a group, are aware of a behavior pattern that is interfering with their effectiveness.

Whom to Involve. The entire group can be involved if the problem has been identified by the group as a whole. If only the facilitators or a few group members have become concerned about a pattern or situation, they can use Go for the Green to analyze it and develop strategies for dealing with it.

Materials Needed. To use Go for the Green, you will need large chart paper and black, green, and red markers.

Tips for Facilitators

Start with a red circle in the middle of the chart paper. Let the group know that you are using that color deliberately because there seems to be a situation that is "making them see red" or is "stopping" them from accomplishing their tasks. Involve the group in deciding on a label to designate the difficult behavior or situation. For example, the team described below was frustrated because team members continually engaged in side conversations and then didn't know what was going on in the discussion. Ideas had to be repeated for them, and time was wasted.

When the problem has been identified in red, switch to the black marker and write across the top of the page "Under what conditions would I . . ." Ask participants to think about reasons they might exhibit that behavior themselves. While they are thinking, switch to the green marker. As they share their thoughts, record them in green on diagonal lines going out from the red circle, like rays on a child's drawing of the sun.

Once the possible causes have been recorded, urge the group to "go for the green" rather than rave about the red. Talk about the various causes and how they might be changed or what accommodations could be made to decrease them.

Two aspects of this technique reduce conflict. By thinking about "why I might . . . ," critics who have complained usually realize that they've been guilty of the same behavior at some point. By going for the green, group members and facilitators often recognize ways in which their own planning (or lack of planning) has contributed to the difficulty.

For Example:
Side Conversations

The leaders of the team were frustrated because it seemed as if they could never get anything completed in the time available for team meetings. Certain combinations of team members would sit together and engage in side conversations throughout the meeting. When their attention returned to the discussion at hand, they would ask people to repeat their statements. If the chairperson asked, "Have we reached a decision?" they would emerge and need a summary of what had transpired and what the tentative conclusion was. They asked me for some idea of how to handle this problem, and I asked if they had a few minutes to learn a new group process technique. They were eager for a new tool, and I conducted a quick Go for the Green activity with them. Figure 7.2 shows the result.

They looked at it for a while and asked if this was what I thought they should do with the group. I said they might want to use it at some time but asked them to look at it again and see if it gave them any ideas of things they might try first. They ended up with a list of strategies that matched the possible causes:

◆ Changing the room configuration so everyone could be around the same table

◆ Guiding the "side conversers" to other seats by setting up name cards on tables before the meeting

◆ Allocating a few minutes at the start of the agenda for participants to "check in" and focus on the purpose of the meeting

◆ Having a timekeeper monitor the agenda

◆ Calling on these participants for their viewpoints early in the discussion of each topic

The concerned participants decided to try these strategies first without confronting the behavior in the whole group. If that didn't work, they were going to ask me to do a Go for the Green and some other work on meeting behavior with their team. They didn't need to call.

Build a Culture of Inquiry

The rhetoric of the 1990s included phrases such as school of learners, learning community, lifelong learning, and collaborative inquiry. All these indicate a need for educators to model the motivation and skills of continued study and professional growth. This book was designed around a set of questions to convey that school change occurs through continuing cycles of inquiry: asking critical questions, seeking answers, proposing and testing solutions, and refining and renewing the process.

It is in the nature of books to start with a Chapter 1 and end after some sequence of content has been presented. The process of change and improvement is not that linear. It is cyclical but even more complex than a single cycle. At any given time, members of the organization may be engaged in studies of several aspects of the school or district. A more accurate visual image of continuous improvement is a corkscrew or Slinky toy, which consists of a series of spirals.

Action research is presented in this chapter to emphasize the importance of inquiry in maintaining the momentum of change and improvement. Several writers on action research describe stages of analyzing problems, collecting data, analyzing data, planning action programs, implementing programs, and evaluating the results. By that definition, this entire book describes a process that is continual action research.

FIGURE 7.2. Go for the Green on Side Conversations

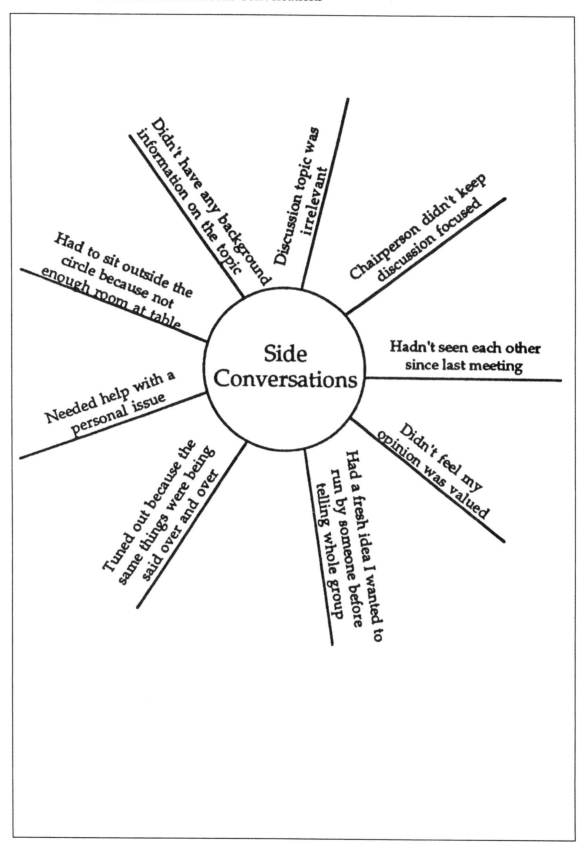

Action Research

Action research is a method of participatory involvement in both individual and group learning. It is one of the few techniques that bridge the individuality of traditional staff development and the common effort of school improvement and organizational development. Action research expands the definition of *teacher* from deliverer of content to scholar of the processes of teaching and learning and investigator of the context of schooling. Participants in action research become more reflective practitioners and are also in a unique position to bridge the gap between K-12 and higher education.

Purpose. Action research is conducted for a number of specific reasons, but the overall purpose is to improve the teaching and learning process in the school. Because participants study topics, problems, or programs related to their roles and interests, action research makes inservice more relevant. Collegial relationships are strengthened, and the likelihood that what participants learn will be accepted by others in the school is increased.

When to Use. Action research is used constantly in a dynamic organization. Gathering data to better understand "Where are we now?" qualifies as action research to many writers. Investigating the possible causes of problems and concerns to decide "Where do we want to go?" and "How will we get there?" also qualifies as action research to some. Experts with the most rigorous definitions of action research place it in the context of piloting a new approach or program and evaluating whether it is working as well as intended or better than other practices. Because this book is written for active practitioners looking at real problems in their schools in the most timely and practical ways, I believe that all these activities qualify as action research.

Whom to Involve. The literature on action research describes three forms: individual, collaborative, and schoolwide. This book outlines a schoolwide process guided by a leadership team, in which the scope of the study encompasses the school as a whole, incorporates shareholder input, and develops action plans that affect all members of the organization. Individual action research can be conducted independently by teachers trying something new within their own classrooms. Collaborative action research involves members of the school staff working as peers. It may also include support and participation by district-level staff and university or college partners. Decisions about who should be involved will emerge when the action research question has been clearly stated and the audience for the findings has been identified.

Materials Needed. Materials needed vary greatly based on the purpose of the action research. They may include literature to review, technical support to gather and analyze data, or additional instructional materials to use with new teaching strategies.

Tips for Facilitators

One of the purposes and benefits of action research is to switch the ownership for change and improvement to the participants within the organization. To achieve this purpose, the role of the facilitator should be advisory and supportive, not central to the effort. As a "guide on the side," a facilitator can assist in important ways.

First, ask probing questions to help the individual or group frame the research problem or question accurately and specifically. The statement "I want to see if cooperative learning really works" is a signal that such guidance is needed. Second, emphasize the need to gather appropriate data from which to draw conclusions. Third, discuss the purpose, methods, and data for the study to be sure that they are congruent.

Also, identify needs for outside expertise and enlist support. For example, if an action research project will include quantitative data analysis, it may be important to include a district-level or university partner as consultant or team member. When deciding whether to pursue a university partnership, remember that a faculty member's reward system is based on conducting research that can be published. In many settings, professors are vulnerable if they spend too much time working with schools in a service capacity. No matter how dedicated they are to supporting the public schools, they will be most interested in projects that address general questions applicable to all schools, are grounded in a particular theory base, and involve rigorous use of data. If these are characteristics of your action research project, it would be wise to seek a higher education partnership. If your focus is primarily internal and pragmatic, expertise from the district or an intermediate service agency may be more appropriate.

Finally, consider the audience for the results of the project. If an individual teacher wants to see whether certain rewards he or she offers will increase the completion of homework assignments, that teacher is the only audience. If a teaching strategy or concept such as learning styles is being piloted by one group of teachers with the intent of testing it for possible schoolwide adoption, the audience is much broader, and the considerations are more complex. As a facilitator or coach, help the project participants anticipate the questions that will be asked by other staff members and be sure that the project will address them.

For Example: Cooperative Learning

Teachers in a junior high school were concerned about poor attendance patterns of their students. They discussed possible reasons for poor attendance at length. About the same time, some of them had been reading about student engagement in learning. A few others had attended a workshop on cooperative learning. They felt that use of cooperative learning might increase achievement and might seem more engaging to the students. Social studies teachers decided to work together and develop cooperative learning activities. Their goal was to have a cooperative learning activity every Thursday and see what would happen.

The data-gathering aspect of their project was overlooked at the time but eventually became an "aha!" event for the entire school. After a month or so, the guidance counselor reported at a faculty meeting that for some reason, school attendance in the seventh and eighth grades was showing an increase and was higher on Thursdays than any other day of the week. He wondered if anyone was doing anything special on Thursdays. When the social studies teachers mentioned their experiment, the language arts teachers decided to test it further. They chose Tuesday as a day to use cooperative learning and consciously set out to have the counselor help them trace the attendance patterns. At the time I lost contact with this school, they had not yet determined the effects on student achievement, but they had certainly made an impact on student interest and stimulated discussion throughout the school.

Refocus and Reaffirm Organizational Values

Growth, change, improvement—these are easy words, but hard work. Only our intrinsic values keep us dedicated to a cause that is difficult and unending. All of us have seen great programs come and go, not because they didn't have good results but because we got tired and returned to old ways that were not actually better—they were just easier.

In our personal lives, most of us would admit the tendency to get so caught up in the demands of our daily lives that we lose touch with our own values. In moments of stress, we hear ourselves say things or find ourselves doing things that are completely out of sync with our own ideals and beliefs. We discover we're driving just as rudely as everyone else in our city. We can't remember the last time we thought about our personal faith or the philosophy of education we brought to our work years ago. Or we realize we are not doing things—such as "random acts of kindness"—that we do consider important and that we want our students, peers, and families to value. Sometimes we wonder how we got into such a state.

Just like individuals, organizations lose touch and lose their way when there is no time to reflect on the meaning of what we do each day. Dynamic organizations constantly reaffirm their organizational values and mission. Some ways to maintain this focus include reflective study groups; conscious decisions about abandoning, synthesizing, integrating, or rejecting current and new practices; and public celebration of organizational achievements.

Reflective Study Groups

The earlier discussion of action research has many features in common with this description of reflective study groups. People doing action research are sometimes called study groups, project teams, quality teams, or site councils. The more important word in this setting is *reflective*. These are small groups of persons who want more from staff development than "getting something new I can use in class tomorrow." These are members of the organization who want to think about implications and concerns and consistency with goals. They are small groups who may meet during lunch once a week, for breakfast on the way to school, or in other environments they choose. They exist for a semester at a time, or they may go on and on. If they have not evolved in your school or district, they need to be initiated and nurtured because they are vital to the soul of the organization.

Purpose. Reflective study groups fulfill many purposes. They contribute to development of new knowledge bases within the school. They raise awareness of needs within the organization and provide feedback by pointing out discrepancies between practice and stated beliefs. Reflective study groups engage in a high level of professional dialogue that is similar to peer coaching. They study new literature and discuss its merits. They encourage each other to try new practices. Perhaps their most unique characteristic is that they challenge each other with probing questions about their experiences. What happened? How and why? What feelings were created? What possible alternatives could be proposed? What plans could we suggest for next time?

When to Use. Reflective study groups can be formed and perform successfully when a climate of trust has been established between the participants and within the organization. Participants within the study group need to establish norms that anything may be questioned but that the questions are not judgmental and that specific conversations are confidential. Decisions about communicating information and feedback to the whole school are made jointly and phrased objectively before being passed along.

Whom to Involve. A rule of thumb on appropriate size for reflective study groups is three to seven participants. At the beginning, members of the group should be individuals with some common interests and prior experience working together as a foundation for the trust level that is essential. Thinking or learning style should be considered as well. With my apologies for this oversimplification, it appears that the concrete, linear thinkers do best or are most comfortable on action research teams with a specific design, whereas the more abstract thinkers contribute greatly to the process of reflection.

Materials Needed. Reflective study groups often begin as ways for colleagues to share things that they have read and learned and to get reactions from each other. Multiple copies of articles or books may be needed for this purpose. As study groups begin to focus on practices within the school and compare them with the best practices and new developments they read about, they may need access to various types of data and assistance interpreting them. One of the most important resources they will need is access to the ears of leadership as they identify new ideas and areas for possible improvement within the school.

Tips for Facilitators

A key role of the facilitator is to establish the norms of respect and confidentiality within the study group. You may be asked to help the group identify a theme for its study, acquire and assemble materials, organize meeting times, record main points made by the group, and provide guidance about how to share the group's new knowledge and ideas with the rest of the staff. It is unusual for all staff members to look on the work of reflective study groups as relevant and irresistible, so prepare them for and help them deal with staff reactions and resistance.

For Example: Lunch Bunch

Years ago, some colleagues and I formed what I believe constituted a reflective study group although it did not emerge as a planned entity according to the suggestions given here. There just happened to be a bunch of us who belonged to the Association for Supervision and Curriculum Development and received its journal, *Educational Leadership,* every month. One day, we were lamenting about how hard it was to keep up with our professional reading and know how to share it with the rest of the school. This was before I knew anything about cooperative learning jigsaws, but we decided to divide up the contents each time, read our articles, and "sneak" over to McDonald's for lunch 1 day per week and talk about them. Others became curious about what we were doing and asked us to give them summaries of good information we found. Although we had no formal role, I believe we contributed to the learning of the organization.

Variations

Some study groups have tried to select excellent articles and make copies to put in everyone's mailbox, but they have been disappointed with the lack of reaction to them. Other groups have told me about two strategies that seem to work better. Rather than distributing the whole article, they prepare a summary on a 3" × 5" card that they distribute. They mention that the full article is posted in several key places in the school and invite anyone interested to talk to one of them about it or meet with them for breakfast on an appointed day.

Staff from another school told me about how they post an article on a large piece of bulletin board paper in the lounge. They highlight the main points so it can be rapidly skimmed, and they hang markers beside it. Casual readers leave "graffiti" comments about the article, which prompt others to read and react as well. The informal reaction energizes the thinking of the staff and sometimes generates ideas for consideration that are brought to the school leadership team and then presented to the whole faculty.

Abandon, Synthesize, Integrate, or Reject

There is a grave danger in learning too much about too many new things. The danger is that we can't do them all and still maintain the degree of focus that is needed to move the whole organization forward together. The effective schools work of Ron Edmonds and Larry Lezotte used the phrase "organized **abandon**ment" to describe a process of looking carefully at existing practices and discontinuing those that are neither effective nor consistent with the values of the organization.

Another way to keep the organization focused is to be sure that similar projects and programs are **synthesize**d into a common effort. Especially at the district level, a function of organizational development is to "let the right hand know what the left hand is doing" and merge their efforts. For example, I once attended a principals' meeting where one of the curriculum specialists described a computer program he had set up to keep textbook inventory and how principals should handle "loaning" textbooks from building to building to maintain an accurate inventory. The audience did not seem appreciative of his efforts. Later, I learned that there was already a software system for keeping track of textbooks that had been developed by the media and technology division. These two projects needed to be synthesized and simplified so that principals could focus on their organization's core values of teaching and learning.

A third way to maintain the focus of the organization is to **integrate** multiple plans into one comprehensive master plan that can be displayed, referred to frequently, and monitored continuously. This is illustrated on Figure 2.1, where multiple action plans for implementation are combined into one master plan under the question "How will we sustain focus and momentum?"

One school filled a huge bulletin board in its foyer with the components from Figure 2.1. Staff members created a beautiful poster of their mission statement and displayed it on the top left corner of the bulletin board. In the lower left corner, they posted the executive summary of their conclusions from analysis of the data in their school portfolio. The priority goals they set were lettered in calligraphy on sentence strips. Strategies for each goal were connected by strings of yarn, which gave them the ability to connect several strategies to more than one goal area. Their combined master plan was illustrated with a series of laminated monthly calendars that highlighted the events from their action plans.

Any visitor to this school knew what was happening and why. Any new idea or grant opportunity had to pass the acid test of proving where it would fit on that crowded, colorful bulletin board.

"Asking the right questions" also applies to deciding whether it's feasible to integrate some new initiative or program or grant opportunity that sounds attractive. The following questions have proved helpful for that purpose:

- What are the underlying values and beliefs of this project or organization?

- Do they fit ours?

- What outcomes are desired by these consultants or vendors or grant donors?

- Are they the outcomes we have already stated we want to achieve?

- What evidence is there that this works to achieve those outcomes?

- What steps, activities, and tasks are required to participate in this?

- Do we have committees or processes that already do that?

Dealing with aggressive vendors who have the perfect program to fit all your needs is sometimes like playing poker. You have to be able to call their bluff. Ask them about their values, beliefs, outcomes, and research before you tell them what *yours* are. A good salesperson is skilled at finding out what your needs are and using your own rhetoric as reassurance that the product will do the trick. Be proactive and prepared to outsmart the vendors who come to your door.

If a new initiative or program can't be integrated into what you're already set to do, the answer is simple—reject, reject, **reject.** This is true even of grants. If new money is going to create new work and make you less effective at what you're already trying to implement, you can't afford it. On the other hand, if the grant-funded activity can help you achieve your goals more effectively than what you're presently doing, or if you're faced with an inescapable mandate, then it's back to the beginning of this section. What can you abandon to make room within organizational capacity for this wonderful new thing?

Dedicate Time

When we define organizational capacity, the least alterable resource on the list is *time,* and the most frequent response when people are asked about barriers to change is *time.* Maintaining focus and momentum means dedicating time to them and protecting that time from other uses. When the Seattle School District launched its academic standards in spring 1999, it was clearly announced that the Summer Institute when teachers returned in August would be devoted completely to topics that related to the Standards-Based Learning System. Vendors who had given promotional presentations in years past were excluded. Sessions were scheduled for every type of teaching assignment and focused on teachers' roles in implementing standards and providing effective instruction to help students meet them. Superintendent Joseph Olchefske compared the Summer Institute program to Henry Ford's guarantee of any color car you wanted as long as it was black. He said, "You can take a course in anything you want, as long as it's related to standards."

I recently asked a group of principals to share the ways in which they were dedicating time for their school's implementation of standards and academic achievement plans. They shared these ideas:

- Develop multiyear plans. You carry forward the goals you're still working on and just replace those that have been met. It keeps the momentum going.

- Put time frames on all the initiatives and work plans. For example, everything about standards says "1998-2001." That reminds people that we're still working on this, and it's not going to go away.

- Keep the focus on a few main, highly visible priorities.

- Allocate all the staff development time that's in the district calendar for specific activities that are in the action plans.

- Rearrange the schedule so that study groups or action teams have common prep time.

- Reduce the class size at certain periods of the day by creating blocks when everyone is teaching reading and every adult in the school has a reading group.

- Develop a schedule and reserve a certain substitute teacher for several days a month. This gives continuity to students so that some work can be accomplished during the school day.

- Get two or three guest teachers to come on a certain day every month. They spend an hour and a half with each grade level, so those teams can meet.

- Be aware that there are multiple models of professional development, and it isn't just having speakers and workshops. Use the time and money for authentic job-embedded collaborative work.

- If you can't get subs, give stipends. It's not good, but it's better than nothing.

- For the money, take another look at summer. Teachers are much more productive on tasks such as developing curriculum or classroom assessments when they're refreshed and focused.

- Write grants so they *buy* time, not *take* time.

Above all, respect people's time by starting and ending as promised and keeping groups on tasks with clear outcomes. A person's time is one resource that cannot be replaced.

Celebrate

A major emphasis of Chapter 6 was the importance of identifying indicators to monitor and gathering data to verify that an improvement plan is actually being implemented and is achieving the intended results. Those are technical aspects of change and accountability. In this chapter, the emphasis is on sustaining change and improvement as part of the culture of the organization. The indicators and data are just as essential, but for a different purpose.

Most of us are comfortable with the phrase "nothing succeeds like success" and mentally apply it to teaching students at the appropriate level of difficulty so that they will be successful and motivated to keep trying and make further progress. The same phrase and logic apply to organizational change. We can't keep on devoting energy above and beyond the call of duty without evidence that it is getting us somewhere. No school or district has the financial resources to provide extrinsic rewards commensurate with the amount of effort required to keep an organization focused on continuous improvement. We need evidence of progress to celebrate and rejuvenate our own energy.

Terry Deal was one of the first to transfer his work on corporate culture to the context of schools, and any of his writing will be helpful. The work of Michael Fullan and Tom Sergiovanni refers to reculturing and the spiritual element of schools as organizations. When benchmarks are reached or milestones achieved, call on the staff members who love drama, the former cheerleaders, the social organizers, and plan unique ways to celebrate!

For Example: Rainier View Elementary School

Rainier View Elementary School[2] serves a student population in which 210 of 283 qualify for free and reduced lunch. The school currently enrolls 55 bilingual students, 27 Level 3 special education students, and 16 resource students, and at least 6 more are waiting to be assessed. At least 80% of the students are bused from other neighborhoods. Needless to say, the school is highly affected by students with special needs.

Five years ago when Mrs. Cothron L. McMillian-Dickey was named principal, the school had a sad reputation. Students were disorderly, staff members were contentious, and academic achievement was so low that the school had been designated for special attention by the district.

Principal McMillian-Dickey had to start at the foundation to rebuild this school. She worked with parents, staff, and the community on the discipline program and introduced school uniforms to bring a sense of identity and order. She literally rearranged the building, changing classroom assignments so that student traffic flow was more efficient and high-visibility programs such as special education had better proximity to assistance from the office. She also went to work on the instructional program, introducing one-to-one and small-group tutoring programs. Specific tutoring interventions include Sound Partners, Reading Partners,

Thinking Partners, and Phono-Graphix. The district's Team Read program coordinates cross-age tutoring between high school and elementary students.

The school curriculum was aligned to district and state standards, and instructional approaches were studied carefully. The direct instruction model was chosen for all reading programs in kindergarten through second grade. Kindergarten students' primary curriculum is DISTAR. Open Court has been implemented in first through third grade. Special programs such as Title I and Special Education also have mandatory reading curriculum that is the direct instruction model of Corrective Reading. Thus, whether students are in the classrooms with teachers or support staff, their instruction is consistent. Mainstream students make the transition easily because of this common approach.

Improvements in the instructional program began to pay off in the third year. From 1998 to 1999, the school's third graders who took the Iowa Tests of Basic Skills gained 6 normal curve equivalents (NCEs) in reading, 3 NCEs in language, and 11 NCEs in math. On the Washington Assessment of Student Learning (WASL), 25.8% more of the students met standards in math compared with the previous group. There were also gains of 36.9% more students meeting standard in writing, and 24.8% more students meeting standard in reading. The performance of fifth graders on the Direct Writing Assessment improved from 45.1% proficient to 70.4%.

At a district all-administrators' meeting, the superintendent awarded certificates to all principals whose schools improved performance on large-scale assessments. He also gave a big blue ribbon to those who improved on all three types of tests. Principal McMillian-Dickey didn't just hang her blue ribbon in the office. She declared a Blue Ribbon day at her school and held a special celebration for the students. Here are her words:

> Since the students were the ones who earned the Blue Ribbon, we had an assembly just for them. It was the first time we had ever paid for a clown. The clown was excellent, and the students thoroughly enjoyed him. Superintendent Olchefske came and spoke to the students about the importance of reading. Barbara Schaad-Lamphere (chairperson of the school board) also spoke, and so did Jan Kumasaka, the school board member who represents our region. Dr. Rimmer, our chief academic officer, also came and congratulated the students on their progress. Everyone wore a real satin blue ribbon on the right forearm. It was powerful.
>
> Another thing we do for our students is that parents raise the funds to take them on major field trips to celebrate their successful accomplishments during testing. We have our own quarterly assessments that are taken by the whole school, then there are the ITBS, WASL, and DWA. After these major events, we take them to places like a movie. We went to Snow Day at Pacific Place a couple of weeks ago—the whole school, including Head Start. We went to the Spaghetti Factory earlier in the year and to the Puyallup Fair. We have three more celebrations planned—roller skating, Woodland Park Zoo, and the Pacific Science Center.
>
> I would always do these things, not because I think the students would work harder or less hard. I do it because I think it is *important* that they feel good about their *own* successes. This was our tangible way of saying, "You are wonderful people who can accomplish any task with a

great deal of effort." The children have to believe in themselves. They have to want it. We can't pour knowledge into their heads. It's our job to motivate them to learn.

As this account demonstrates, the people at Rainier View know that celebrations are not just about accomplishments already past. Celebrations are about motivation in the present and hope for the future.

Support Leaders and Followers

Organizational change may be an oxymoron like jumbo shrimp. Organizations don't change as whole entities. They change as the people within them do, and those people don't change all at the same time. There are leaders; there are optimistic followers; there are pessimistic, reluctant followers; and there are some who don't budge at all. Those who lead the way—and those who readily join them—need support to weather initial resistance and continue their efforts. They need technical support to help get the actual work done. They also need the psychological and moral support of others who are and have been involved in the same situations.

Technical Support

Improving schools requires two sets of skills that few school leaders have had the opportunity to acquire in their graduate work or have seen modeled in their own experience. The first of these is how to involve others in decision making. The other is how to use data in appropriate ways to guide the decision making. School districts need to provide their leaders with training in teamwork and group process skills and give them access to external facilitators when they need help and encouragement working with groups. Technical support in gathering and analyzing data and access to individuals with the expertise for statistical analysis are essential.

Technical support is also a critical component of any major initiative in a school or district. When the Standards-Based Learning System (SBLS) was introduced in the Seattle School District, clear expectations were set for how principals would support teachers and how the district would support the schools. Principals' support for standards implementation was to include these activities:

- ◆ Know and show teachers how to use the SBLS materials

- ◆ Coordinate time for collaborative planning and scoring

- ◆ Keep the focus on priorities; don't allow distractions

- ◆ Build a core of support and nurture teacher leaders

- ◆ Observe for evidence of the 15 Indicators (see Chapter 6)

- ◆ Engage all adults and hold everyone accountable

- ◆ Align Academic Achievement Plan with standards and assessment priorities

- Promote, model, and teach use of data

- Address school climate issues from an academic perspective

The district, in turn, outlined its support for standards implementation in these ways:

- Offer SBLS classes at a variety of locations and times

- Provide a team of support specialists[2] who will come to schools and

  - Answer questions at staff meetings

  - Teach models of standards-based lessons

  - Observe in classrooms and provide feedback

  - Facilitate collaborative planning and scoring of student work

- Maintain the Standards Network so teachers can meet and share

- Continue to align the instructional program (e.g., report card revision)

- Communicate answers to questions and new information through newsletters

- Produce videotapes and materials for use in school-based but district-wide staff development

- Maintain the focus on this initiative for several years so it will really happen

The third type of coaching I mentioned in Chapter 6 involves my role with the cadre of standards support specialists who work with teachers and principals on a regular basis.[3] These are teachers who came directly from the classroom, so their range of coaching and facilitation skills varied depending on each person's prior experiences. We didn't have the luxury of a long retreat to practice our roles or bring in a consultant for Training of Trainers, so I coached their skills in small segments at our weekly staff meetings. Initially, we spent time role-playing situations they were encountering and asking for advice about how to handle them. Scenarios were introduced, such as a conflict between a principal and teacher regarding standards implementation. I played the role of the teacher while one of the standards support specialists responded to the concerns and the other team members provided feedback. Role playing was an effective way to help them learn strategies for dealing with conflict.

We also spent time discussing and developing concrete examples of the 15 Indicators of SBLS (Chapter 6). This included creating a standards-based unit and presenting it to a colleague. Explaining their planning process helped solidify their own understanding and provided mental rehearsal for the questions they would be asked at schools. As we debriefed on various sessions with school and community groups, we improved presentation skills and developed a format for all workshop planning that included a standard for amount of presenter time and participant engagement time.

During a span of 8 months, I experienced the thrill of a coach who can observe the process as individuals develop personal skills and also grow as an interdependent team. That's the best part of being a coach—but also the worst part. The better you coach, the faster they grow, the sooner you become nonessential. Now the coached are the coaches, and the Standards Network planning and facilitating are almost completely in their hands.

Networking

School districts need to coordinate collegial support for their leaders. Access to e-mail as a quick, informal way to communicate within the district and with more distant colleagues should be provided to every principal encountering new challenges of school change. Designating and coordinating mentor relationships is another form of networking that should occur through the district or professional associations. Just assigning a mentor is inadequate. Someone needs to be instrumental in setting times and places for mentors to communicate, helping them focus on needs and questions, and keeping the network active.

Teachers need networks, too. Classrooms are often places of isolation, and a school across town is sometimes as foreign as a school across the county or country. The Standards Network mentioned earlier has evolved to have a powerful role connecting the 100+ schools in the district. When three to five teachers come from each school, it is sometimes a unique experience just to be together with their own team members. When they reconfigure into grade-level groups that include colleagues from other schools, they get new ideas and energy. When they take materials and tasks back to their school for reflection and follow-up, they strengthen the communication loop between the district and the schools and among the schools across the district. Instead of a hierarchy of district committees to deal with things such as report card revision, this network provides a way to engage every teacher throughout the district who is interested in providing input.

The concept of networking has emerged in two other ways in the Seattle district. Earlier in this book, I described the district cuts and site-based approach to curriculum that resulted in a wide variety of reading philosophies and approaches in the district. As more schools have made budget decisions to staff a part- or full-time reading specialist in their building, it became possible to develop a Reading Network. Through this network, reading specialists are learning about best practices in other schools and gaining new insights for their roles in their schools.

I have also referred to the transformation of our corps of middle school principals brought about through the leadership of Director Aimee Hirabayashi. A small grant provided enough resources for these 10 principals to network at dinner once a month. The interaction, the relaxation of eating, and the opportunity to meet away from the school day and site provided more than just physical fuel. The food for thought stimulated interactions between schools and initiated the middle school conference described in Chapter 5.

Active Listening

I recently worked with a principal who divided her time between three tiny, geographically remote schools. We talked about the uniqueness of her schools, and I asked her about her needs and ways the district could better assist her. She gave me a wistful look like that of a child staring through the window of a candy store, and I wondered whether I had created an expectation so great I'd surely fail to meet it. But with a sigh, all she said was, "What I need most is someone to talk to about all this, but I guess that's not the district's job. I guess it's a personal problem." She was both right and wrong. It is something she needs, and it is something the district should provide. Because her schools are different from the others in the system, she hadn't been able to find a mentor among her peers. She has one now.

Purpose. In addition to having a specific person to share questions and concerns with, principals and other school leaders need opportunities to practice their own listening skills and interact with a wider range of colleagues. I first learned about a group process called Active Listening Trios from friends in the California School Leadership Academy. I have seen it adapted by several facilitators for use in a variety of other settings.

When to Use. This group activity for active listening can be repeated every few months, focused on a common concern most relevant at that time. It can also be used after training in a new technique to identify and respond to concerns about implementation.

Whom to Involve. One or more groups of three people who are willing to give each other 45 minutes of caring time are needed. The process can be used to increase communication and understanding among groups of teachers, within school leadership teams, in adult-student interactions, and even in families.

Materials Needed. Active Listening Trios need a topic or concern as a focus and a timer to move the process along.

Tips for Facilitators

Begin by reviewing the characteristics of active listening:

◆ Using positive, open nonverbals

◆ Paraphrasing

◆ Asking probing questions

◆ Jotting down important points if the speaker consents

◆ Withholding advice until all the information is shared

◆ Hearing advice in full before reacting

Ask participants to form groups of three. There may be times when you structure the composition of the trios. For example, if a workshop setting includes people from several districts, I will encourage mixed groups as an opportunity to share ideas from other areas.

Within the trios, have one person designated as *A*, another as *B*, and the third as *C*. Provide a focus for their conversation, and explain the following steps so they have a grasp of the overall sequence:

Round 1

A shares and explains; *B* and *C* listen with no comment.

B and *C* ask clarifying questions only (no statements); *A* answers.

B and *C* offer advice and suggestions; *A* listens.

Round 2

B shares and explains; *A* and *C* listen with no comment.

A and *C* ask clarifying questions only (no statements); *B* answers.

A and *C* offer advice and suggestions; *B* listens.

Round 3

C shares and explains; *A* and *B* listen with no comment.

A and *B* ask clarifying questions only (no statements); *C* answers.

A and *B* offer advice and suggestions; *C* listens.

Establish a time limit for each step (4 minutes seems to work well), and select an unobtrusive signal for when to move on. Move a marker along an overhead transparency to provide a silent reminder of what to do next. Ask them to stay with the process even if they can't think of any more to say at that step. Remind them of the importance of "wait time" to let both speakers and listeners process at a deeper level.

After the exercise has been completed, encourage participants to share

◆ What they learned about their problem and about listening in general

◆ How it felt to be listened to without interruption for 4 minutes

◆ How it felt to be silent and not interrupt for 4 full minutes

◆ How they might use this exercise in other settings

For Example: Family Fun

I conducted the Active Listening Trios exercise among a group of principals who responded to the prompt "My biggest concerns about shared decision making are . . ." The activity was well received, the participants discovered that they had many of the same concerns, they generated good strategies for dealing with them, and several made commitments to keep in touch and marked dates in their calendars to establish a set time for communication.

A few weeks later, I unexpectedly encountered one of the participants in a shopping mall. He said, "You're the one who did the listening thing, right?" I agreed, and he went on to tell me how he and his wife had used the same process with a teenager in their home. He told me how embarrassed they were to discover that they had never spent even 4 whole minutes listening to his viewpoint on anything and how much mutual respect had been gained as all three of them got equal time to share their feelings. They used this technique to turn family feuds into family fun.

In this chapter, we have explored the question of "How will we sustain the focus and momentum?" Whether we create organizations that examine themselves and pursue continuous improvement depends, in large part, on how we treat those who carry the load on a daily basis. A most important aspect of leadership is nurturing the human resources of the organization through technical support, active listening, and caring responses.

Notes

1. During the production of this second edition, Cal Ripken, Jr. provided further evidence of focus and momentum—becoming the 23rd member of the 3000 Hit Club.

2. For more information about Rainier View Elementary School, e-mail Principal McMillian-Dickey (cmcmill@cks.ssd.k12.wa.us).

3. Our standards support coaches are Gary Cranston, Jane Goetz, Joani Harr, and Wendy Cornacchio (e-mail addresses are gcranston, jgoetz, jharr, and wcornacchio followed by @seattleschools.org).

8

Bonus Questions

Somewhere I heard that "no one likes change except a wet baby." The five critical questions examined in Chapters 3 through 7 guide the process of school improvement. The bonus questions presented in this chapter address some of the effects of change on participants and observers.

Travelers on the road to school improvement know that it is going to be a long trip with twists and turns and bumps along the way. But there are two things they should not have to experience. Their confidence should not be daunted or their past efforts demeaned. A danger with initiating change for the future is that it can feel to the "changees" like an accusation that everything they have done before is somehow wrong. The bonus questions "Did it make sense then?" and "Does it make sense now?" can be used to affirm the value of prior experience before moving into a new phase.

Traveling alone is no fun either. The need for networks and support was stressed in Chapter 7. The bonus question "Who else?" encourages leaders to draw on the knowledge and interest of others and challenges us to accept our critical leadership role.

Did It Make Sense Then?
Does It Make Sense Now?

A powerful phrase in the vocabulary of the 1980s was "paradigm shift." We all learned that a paradigm was an attitude or predisposition that governs our behavior, a perception held so strongly that it might not even be conscious, a filter through which we interpret everything around us. Our paradigms determine what we will consider right and possible. Sometimes we get so locked into our paradigms that we suffer from "paradigm paralysis." The terminology was so overused that it became discounted as another fad. In one workshop I attended, a group member said, "I wouldn't give you two cents for this stuff, let alone a pair o'dimes."

Although the terminology became cliché, the concept is an essential one. We have inherited and absorbed attitudes from our past experience that are so strong we may not know they exist. We have never questioned them because we are unaware of them. We just know that we get uncomfortable with some new ideas that "just don't feel right." Some groups have found it helpful to start "letting go" by identifying things that have *not* changed about schools in the past 50 to 100 years. Some of the items that appear on a typical list are the following:

◆ 9 months of school

◆ Dismissing about 3:00

◆ Grade levels

◆ Carnegie units for high school graduation

◆ Self-contained elementary classrooms

◆ Departmentalized secondary schools

◆ A, B, C, D, and F grades

◆ Separate tracks for college-bound and vocational students

The next step is to revisit those structures of schooling with the question "Did it make sense then?" The 9-month school year gets linked to an agricultural economy, and we ask, "Did it make sense then?" The answer is yes. So—good for us! Why did we dismiss school about 3:00? The answer that eventually emerges is "because factories ran a day shift that got out about 3:00." Did it make sense in the industrial period? Yes? Well, good for us! What about Carnegie units? Where did they come from? Many people don't know that Carnegie pioneered the effort to identify some common standards as prerequisites that would put students on a more even playing field when they went on to a higher level of education. Did it make sense in the days of rural schools to give them something to shoot for? Yes. Then good for us as public educators! Conduct similar conversations for the other items on the list and emphasize that those practices didn't emerge just by happenstance. They were responses to the needs of society—the shareholders—at that time. Encourage the participants to congratulate themselves and brag to each other about how public education was customer oriented even before that adjective was used.

When the celebration of pride dies down, pause and ask softly, "Does it make sense now?" Many groups act a little stunned by the question, but then they begin acknowledging that we do many things based on tradition, without thought about whether they still fit. They are also reassured when they realize that aspects of schooling we took for granted were once reforms themselves based on the needs of a changing society.

Use of these two questions will not lead to overnight restructuring and will not make the change process itself any easier. But these questions can help groups become more conscious of the origins of our traditions while reasserting pride in our past experience. From there, they can move on to preserving the things that still make sense and considering ways to change the things that don't. At the least, it's a far more positive experience than sitting in an auditorium for 3 hours while a zealot with a new cause castigates and humiliates us for being so outdated and so far behind every other decent country in the world.

Who Else . . . Should Be Included?

Organizations change as people within them change. That's one reason for the emphasis on participation and involvement in the study and planning phases of school improvement. Another reason is that organizational change is far too difficult and complex for one leader to be able to make it happen.

A veteran principal who was trying to make his own paradigm shift from benevolent dictator to a more shared approach discovered that he needed constant reminders to include others. In his wallet, on his daily calendar, and above the door inside his office, he placed the two words *Who Else?* When he analyzed a situation and prepared to "share decisions" by announcing what he had decided, those signs were his prompts to think about who else should have a voice. They would remind him to consider who else might have expertise to share, who else would be affected by the decision, and above all, whose cooperation was essential to making the decision work. By concentrating on these visual reminders, the experienced principal found himself receiving compliments from parents and staff on his new leadership style.

Who Else . . . If Not Me?

Throughout the quality improvement literature, there are references to how 80% of the work in an organization is done by 20% of the people. Sometimes it seems as if the improvement work in schools is done by only 2% of the people, and in an organization of 100 members, that 2% may feel like "me and my secretary." When we are discouraged and fatigued and tempted to ask "Why me?" we need to answer a question with a question: "Who else . . . if not me?" If I don't model perseverance, who else will? If I don't have the emotional intelligence to understand and manage my own emotions, motivate myself, and demonstrate empathy and interpersonal effectiveness, who else will model it for the adolescents in our care? If I don't model continuous personal improvement, who else will care about continual professional and organizational improvement? If I don't reach out to meet our constituents halfway, who else will see the need to do so? The "Who else?" question can be a powerful tool in our own self-talk and motivation as leaders.

9

Using This Book

Asking the Right Questions was conceived from a marriage of critical questions and group process techniques for teams to use to answer them. They have been organized into a matrix and offered as an aid for team leaders, facilitators, and consultants. My goal was that they be helpful in some of the following ways.

As a Quick Index to Your Toolbox

In Chapter 1, I described an out-of-the-blue request for advice on how to handle a group process challenge. You probably have those experiences, too, and you are probably familiar with most or all these group process techniques. They are already "in your toolbox."

Once I was asked to facilitate an activity but was cautioned, "no flip charts and no circles." I was happy to agree, but curious. It turned out that a consultant on a long-term contract with the district had only one tool in his toolbox—get in a circle, no writing instruments or surfaces allowed, and reach consensus on everything including the color of marker he should use to write on the flip chart. Sometimes we get into a pattern of using one technique over and over and forget some of the others we have enjoyed using and found to be effective in other settings. One use of this matrix is to help us quickly scan the tools we have, so that we can select one that will match the task before us.

When asked to facilitate an activity, get enough information to know what question the participants are trying to answer. Are they figuring out where they are now? Are they trying to set a goal? Are they deciding how to get there? Or are they simply struggling with some natural conflicts that are part of change and growth? Find their question on the left and move across the matrix to choose one of the group process techniques that address their need.

You have also developed skills that I didn't include in this book. Print the matrix on a larger sheet of paper and add columns on the right for techniques you enjoy using. Think about the range of applications they have for answering the five critical questions. Place your own Xs in the cells of the matrix, and you have an even bigger toolbox than mine.

As a Tool for Planning Personal Skill Development

As you have read this book, you may have recognized every group process technique described. If so, skip this paragraph. If some of the activities were new to you, I'd suggest that you start like this. Get a highlighting pen and go across the top of the matrix. Highlight each technique you come to that you have used before and are confident you could facilitate with others. Go down each of those columns with the highlighter. Now you have a colored matrix to serve as a quick index to your own toolbox. You also have some "white spaces." These are the group process techniques you may wish to add to your toolbox. Consult the annotated bibliography and read more about them, find a workshop that includes them, or seek out a mentor who is willing to coach you as you practice them. This adds to your repertoire of skills and lets you color in more of the matrix as you develop new strategies.

As a Tool for Designing Team Training

Chapter 7 points out the importance of continued training to sustain the focus and momentum of change. One of the concepts mentioned is just-in-time training. This concept is particularly true for group process techniques. The prevalent pattern of sending a group of people to a conference on teamwork leaves many feeling as though they accomplished little real work, and transfer to their own setting is limited.

A more effective way to learn about teamwork is in the context of the immediate tasks that need to be accomplished. When you are asked to "give us some training in group techniques" or "teach us some strategies to use on our team," first get information on what the purpose of the team is and what tasks the participants are now trying to accomplish. Use the matrix to identify techniques team members can use for the task at hand and design the content of their training to introduce techniques they can apply immediately. Provide time for them to plan how and when they will use the new technique and facilitate it with each other.

The Kentucky Leadership Academy used this book in a problem-based learning approach to team training. Figure 9.1 shows a handout from their materials. Participants were divided into groups and chose or were assigned one of the scenarios. They talked about how they could assist a group in this situation, chose one of the group process techniques, and talked each other through how they would facilitate it. Then they returned to their home teams and shared what they had learned and planned. This helped entire teams expand their repertoire. It also provided a comfortable way for them to share situations they were facing and ask for input and advice from others in the group.

FIGURE 9.1. A Problem-Based Learning Approach to Team Training

If . . . the following scenario occurs:	**Then** . . . which matrix strategy would you choose?
1. As district leader you have just received the action plan from the schools. You need a method of review. Identify a strategy that could be used to review all school plans.	
2. You are facilitating a districtwide committee and 2 of the 8 elementary schools have identified significant science priority needs. Identify a strategy that could be utilized to facilitate decisions regarding use of district Title II funds.	
3. You have just received your budget allocation from the district office. Your task is to budget your consolidated plan. You don't know how to start this process. Identify a strategy that could be used for beginning this process.	
4. You have a committee that has identified key findings, and they are ready to prioritize needs. The committee begins to ignore the data gathered through the needs assessment and begins to establish priority needs based upon beliefs not supported by data. Identify a strategy that could be used to complete the task.	
5. The language art teachers are developing an action plan but have not completed the plan because they cannot agree upon specific activities to reach component objectives. Three teachers want to improve reading through implementation of whole language strategies, and three teachers want to use direct instruction materials. Identify a strategy that could be implemented to resolve this conflict.	
6. Create your own scenario. . . .	

As a Tool for Coaching
New Facilitators

The matrix can also be helpful as you work with cadres of internal trainers or as you coach new facilitators. Have them highlight the columns of the matrix under skills with which they feel comfortable. This provides a starting point. You can observe your facilitators using those techniques to check their skill and provide feedback to help them refine their approaches. When you are also confident of their expertise in these areas, they can become coaches for others.

Also look at the white spaces they have not highlighted. Go across the matrix horizontally. If there is a whole section—one of the five critical questions—that is mostly white, start their new learning with a group process technique that will begin to fill in that gap.

As a Tool for Diagnosing
Your Status and Process

It's hard to believe that it's been 17 years since I began my own journey facilitating school improvement. The research on effective schools was quite new, the roles of principals and teachers were quite well defined, and the schools were conducted primarily according to decisions made at the district level. For several years, I worked with schools that were "blank slates." They had little prior history, and I could present the school improvement process as a relatively straightforward, step-by-step approach.

Then came a proliferation of different approaches to school and district planning, which led to the situation described in Scenario 2. It became much more difficult to work with a school. First I would have to figure out their vocabulary and their model and adapt accordingly.

Now there are chaos theory and complexity theory and "flow," and schools are not at the *beginning* of anything—they're right in the middle of a whole maelstrom of swirling processes and initiatives and new mandates. So Figure 2.1 probably can't be used in the sort of "start here and follow the yellow brick road" way that I've written the book. After all, you have to write things down in some type of sequence, even when you know that real life is not that rational or linear.

I do believe, and have discovered time and again, that a visual organizer such as Figure 2.1 can be useful to help people who are in the middle of the swirl rise above it and look down and see the various parts of what's going on and make much better sense of the big picture. So . . . where to start? Start *anywhere* that's a place where people are interested. If you already have strategies, but no action plans, start there. If you have a lot of data, but nobody's looked at them to see what they mean, sit down with the data and brainstorm the list of concerns that arise in the conversation.

Start *somewhere*. School change may be "like pushing on the end of a string," but if you find someone at the other end who's willing to pull, just two of you can begin on that issue together.

On the other hand, you may discover, as Principal Stephanie Haskins did, that you have to start *everywhere*.

For Example:
Madison Middle School

Madison Middle School[1] serves 890 students in grades 6 through 8 in a diverse, blue-collar area of the city. When Stephanie Haskins became principal in 1996, the school had low staff morale coupled with universal dissatisfaction with the direction and organization of the school indicated on staff surveys. Many parents were also indicating that they were unhappy with the school because their survey ratings came in well below district averages. Even students had negative feelings toward the school. Their surveys indicated that they were scoring well below district average in the areas of student relations, safety, staff-student relations, and learning climate.

Stephanie is a systems thinker, and she realized that it was going to be impossible to start in just one place. Student achievement is related to attendance, so how can you work on achievement without working on attendance? Students don't learn in disorderly environments, so how can you work on learning without working on order and safety? Teachers don't function at their best when they lack a sense of efficacy, so how can you improve instruction without increasing empowerment? It just went on and on.

So Ms. Haskins worked with the staff to identify all the systems that needed to be aligned:

- Attendance
- Discipline
- Budget planning
- Operating principles
- Student intervention
- Student health
- Master calendar coordination
- Curriculum delivery
- Cultural diversity
- Master schedule design
- Shared decision making
- Safety/emergency preparedness
- Site council/PTA
- Communications/public relations
- Student-teacher activities planning and incentives
- General operations including office support
- Staff development

Then Madison Middle School started *everywhere*—on 17 things at once. Seventeen study groups were established, and as they worked out the kinks in the system they were assigned, the material went into a staff handbook, the study group was discontinued, and the leadership team took over monitoring the system. As these systems came on line, more people became available to look at issues of teaching and learning. The combined work of these study groups is compiled in the Staff Handbook and Academic Achievement Handbook, which are the most valuable documents of this type I have seen.

Teachers at Madison Middle School have implemented schoolwide rubrics so students know that there are common expectations for work acceptable by all teachers. A critical thinking curriculum outlines thinking skills and advance organizers for students to add to their repertoire at each grade level. Madison's challenge curriculum is based on inclusion, so that all students who want to tackle more rigorous learning experiences have that opportunity. There are team planning forums and "escalation" plans to fast-forward the progress of students not on track to be ready for high school.

It must be working. The percentage of students achieving standards on the state assessment has increased in all areas of reading, writing, math, and listening. Direct Writing Assessment results exceed the district average. All survey measures have improved significantly so that the school rates well above district averages by students, staff, and parents. Madison staff members give presentations around the state and host visitors from inside and outside the district. As energy that had been soaked up by dysfunctional adult systems became redirected toward student learning, all this was accomplished in just 3 years.

Madison is now characterized by whole school, student-focused thought and action. It's also proof that there's an alternative to the snail's pace of small, incremental steps in the journey of school change.

Blast Off

There are ramblers, and there are travelers. The ramblers will wind up where they will and probably won't remember how they got there. The travelers will probably reach their destination, especially if there are rest stops and information booths along the way. As leaders, change agents, and group facilitators, we staff the rest stops and information booths. If we provide adequate support and accurate guidance, the travelers are more likely to be interested in taking another trip, pursuing yet another destination of improvement.

The ultimate travelers are the astronauts who broke the space barrier and who now make shuttle missions seem almost routine. I remember the first step on the moon, I held my breath with the rest of the country during *Apollo 13*, and I watched the *Challenger* disaster and tried to explain it to my students. So I was anxious to visit the Kennedy Space Center with my husband and three nieces. My most powerful memory is of the Mission Control room, where I watched in fascination as the green panels lit up to mark the countdown toward launch—and chills went through me as one panel flashed repeatedly, COMMIT—COMMIT—COMMIT. I realized how irrevocable that decision was and thought about the courage of those who had taken that risk. And, as usual, I thought about commitment to school change.

The second highlight of the tour was seeing the shuttle *Columbia* sitting on the launchpad being prepared for the next shuttle mission. The timing was significant because this was to be the first mission with a female commander. My nieces and I reveled in the knowledge that somewhere in a building we passed on the bus, Lieutenant Colonel Eileen Collins was getting ready to make history. She would be responsible for the heaviest and most expensive payload ever: NASA's 25-ton, $1.5 billion Chandra X-ray Observatory. Gina, Kacie, Danielle, and I talked about the importance of their math and science education and physical health and having lofty goals and how much more they would be able to do than my generation or my mother's. And, as usual, I thought about school change—and wondered if their schools have changed enough to deliver on their dreams.

Back home a few days later, I watched the launch of the STS-93 mission. There were moments of anxiety as an electrical short knocked out some computers for the main engines and an instrument display in the cockpit failed. Tiny leaks caused the engines to run out of fuel seconds too soon to reach the exact desired orbit. As commander, Collins remained calm throughout the mission and completed the release of Chandra on schedule with all systems functioning perfectly.

A short time later, I was preparing to leave for the office when I overheard the announcer say that Lt. Col. Collins was to be Katie Couric's next guest on the *Today* show. Having set her up as a role model for my nieces, I wanted to see her and hear what she had to say. Couric asked Collins whether she was afraid when things started going wrong and how she made the decision to continue with the launch.

The answer was simple. This courageous woman said something like this:

> First of all, I didn't have time to be scared. We train so thoroughly and have a plan for everything that my mind was just running through the plan and preparing to do whatever came next. Second, we have total faith in the support teams on the ground who are monitoring every system very carefully and would not put us in harm's way. So—no—I wasn't scared, and it was an easy decision to commit to launch.

The conversation took me back to that moment in the Mission Control simulation when the flashing green panel signaled the moment of no turning back. And, as usual, I thought about school change. Those statements by Lt. Col. Collins sounded like answers to the question of how we get people to commit to school improvement. We need plans. We need training. We must provide plenty of support. Our principals and teachers need to know both that we are monitoring *and* that we won't put them in harm's way.

These are the conditions that replace fear with faith to commit to the shared journey of school change. If we don't have the courage to make that journey, there are young men and women who will never reach the destination of their dreams. God speed us all.

Note

1. Madison Middle School is located at 3429 45th Avenue, S.W., Seattle, WA 98116. Principal Stephanie Haskins can be reached at 206-933-5340 or by e-mail (shaskins@is.ssd.k12.wa.us).

Annotated Bibliography

Anderson, S. E., Rolheiser, C., & Bennett, B. (1995). Confronting the challenge of implementing cooperative learning. *Journal of Staff Development, 16,* 32-38.

This article describes the use of the Stages of Concern Questionnaire to guide implementation of cooperative learning.

Bolman, L. G., & Deal, T. E. (1994). *Becoming a teacher leader: From isolation to collaboration.* Thousand Oaks, CA: Corwin.

This book is based on the authors' previous work describing organizations using the political, structural, human resource, and symbolic frameworks. The concepts are illustrated in story fashion, as two teachers discuss their changing roles.

Bonstingl, J. J. (1992). *Schools of quality: An introduction to total quality management in education.* Alexandria, VA: Association for Supervision and Curriculum Development.

Bonstingl's book provides a bridge between the business approach to quality management and the real world of schools. The appendixes are quick references to tools of quality and Deming's 14 Points.

Bullard, P., & Taylor, B. O. (1994). *Keepers of the dream: The triumph of effective schools.* Lake Forest, IL: Excelsior.

This book tells the stories of successful school reform efforts accomplished through effective schools programs across the United States. The voices of superintendents, principals, teachers, and community members are heard as they describe successful teamwork that changed their schools.

Deal, T. E., & Peterson, K. D. (1999). *Shaping school culture: The heart of leadership.* San Francisco: Jossey-Bass.

This is an expanded version of the best-seller first published by the U.S. Department of Education as The Principal's Role in Shaping School Culture. Deal and

Peterson describe principals as historians, anthropological sleuths, visionaries, symbols, potters, poets, actors, and healers. The most helpful new chapter describes toxic cultures and presents some antidotes for dealing with those strong negative elements that infect and suck the energy out of the working and learning environment.

Evans, R. (1996). *The human side of school change: Reform, resistance, and the real-life problems of innovation.* San Francisco: Jossey-Bass.

Evans's book is presented in three parts: The Nature of Change, Dimensions of Change, and Leading Innovation. The first two parts can be discouraging, and tired school leaders may want to read them last, rather than first. They explore resistance to change in a thorough, sympathetic manner and explain many leadership challenges as natural manifestations of midlife and midcareer realities. Fortunately, the third part of the book provides encouragement and good advice for authentic leaders—who provide clarity and focus, who encourage participation while remaining out in front, who model and stimulate recognition of performance, and who confront serious resistance directly. The sections on site-based management, collaboration, and empowerment are particularly good for principals struggling to be leaders in decentralized environments.

Fullan, M. G. (1993). *Change forces: Probing the depths of educational reform.* New York: Falmer.

This book represents Fullan's next stage of thinking after The Meaning of Educational Change and The New Meaning of Educational Change. Although his previous work was rather technical and focused on structural issues, this book reveals a greater understanding of the complexity of change. Fullan places new emphasis on the importance of moral purpose and development of school culture as a learning organization.

Fullan, M. G. (1999). *Change forces: The sequel.* Philadelphia: Falmer.

Every scholar and practitioner of school leadership should continue to read Fullan's ever evolving work on educational change. With this installment, Fullan stretches beyond the technical, organizational approach to change and delves deeply into the essential aspect of moral purpose. The complexity of creating collaborative cultures is presented as eight lessons that incorporate chaos theory and emotional intelligence and can be applied to collaboration within the school and with community and outside agencies.

Fullan, M. G., & Stiegelbauer, S. M. (1991). *The new meaning of educational change.* New York: Teachers College Press.

This comprehensive look at school change combines research and practical application in a substantive but easily readable style. Discussion of the stages of initiation, implementation, and institutionalization or continuation appear in Chapters 5 and 6. Part II is particularly helpful in school settings, describing the impact of change on teachers, principals, students, district administrators, parents, and communities.

Holcomb, E. L. (1991). *School-based instructional leadership: Staff development for teacher and school effectiveness.* Madison, WI: National Center for Effective Schools.

This multimedia training program includes a participant's notebook, a trainer's notebook, and Training of Trainers materials. It is designed in nine modules for use with cross-role teams of teachers, principals, other staff members, parents, and community members. A section on survey instruments and other resource materials is included. The program is now being distributed by Phi Delta Kappa. For information, contact Phil Harris, Center for Professional Development, PDK, 408 N. Union, Bloomington, IN 47402.

Holcomb, E. L. (1999). *Getting excited about data: How to combine people, passion, and proof.* Thousand Oaks, CA: Corwin.

Expanding on the first edition of Asking the Right Questions, Getting Excited About Data focuses on the need for greater use of data in planning, decision making, and reporting results of change efforts and instructional programs in schools. Unlike most other books about data, which present technical and statistical information, this book emphasizes the human dimension. It includes sections on why teachers are reluctant to look at data, how to address the resistance and motivate interest, and how to bridge the perceived conflict between being student centered and data driven. Several districts and state agencies have adopted Getting Excited About Data as their guidebook for comprehensive school improvement planning and have converted its visuals into templates and CD-ROM format.

Holly, P. (1991). Action research: The missing link in the creation of schools as centers of inquiry. In A. Lieberman & L. Miller (Eds.), *Staff development for education in the '90s: New demands, new realities, new perspectives* (2nd ed., pp. 133-157). New York: Teachers College Press.

Holly provides a scholarly discussion of the historical development of action research and describes the stages of problem formulation, data collection, and data analysis.

Hord, S. M., Rutherford, W. L., Huling-Austin, L., & Hall, G. E. (1987). *Taking charge of change.* Alexandria, VA: Association for Supervision and Curriculum Development.

This book is an essential tool for diagnosing the concerns of individuals in change and helping the organization respond. It provides background information on development of the concerns-based adoption model and the Stages of Concern Questionnaire. Detailed explanations for use of the instrument and interpretation of profiles are included.

Johnson, D. W., & Johnson, F. P. (1994). *Joining together: Group theory and group skills.* Boston: Allyn & Bacon.

This book provides theoretical background on group dynamics, as well as practical advice for improving communication in groups, leading learning and discussion groups, and nurturing team development. The chapter on decision making is especially helpful with its clarification of consensus.

Katz, N. H., & Lawyer, J. W. (1994). *Resolving conflict successfully: Needed knowledge and skills*. Thousand Oaks, CA: Corwin.

The second of three volumes on conflict resolution for school administrators, this book provides helpful information on building rapport, reflective listening, and problem solving.

Lezotte, L., & Jacoby, B. (1990). *A guide to the school improvement process based on effective schools research*. Okemos, MI: Effective Schools Products.

This handbook outlines the school improvement process and provides sample forms, timelines, and practical suggestions for implementation.

Loucks-Horsley, S., & Stiegelbauer, S. M. (1991). Using knowledge of change to guide staff development. In A. Lieberman & L. Miller (Eds.), *Staff development for education in the '90s: New demands, new realities, new perspectives* (2nd ed., pp. 15-36). New York: Teachers College Press.

This chapter provides an overview of the concerns-based adoption model and a description of how to use the Stages of Concern Questionnaire to plan staff development programs.

McManus, A. (1992). *The memory jogger for education: A pocket guide of tools for continuous improvement in schools*. Methuen, MA: GOAL/QPC.

This booklet was adapted from a similar guide for business that was compiled and edited by Michael Brassard. It provides diagrams and brief instructions for use of statistical tools such as histograms, run charts, and control charts.

Scholtes, P. R. (1988). *The team handbook: How to use teams to improve quality*. Madison, WI: Joiner.

This handbook reviews the basics of quality improvement and describes the use of statistical tools for quality improvement. It also includes chapters on forming a project team, guidelines for productive meetings, building improvement plans, and team dynamics. It is helpful for readers who can create their own bridges between the business context and schools.

Taylor, B. O., & Bullard, P. (1995). *The revolution revisited: Effective schools and systemic reform*. Bloomington, IN: Phi Delta Kappa.

This small booklet is filled with a collection of reports that update the development of the effective schools process in schools nationwide. The comprehensive systemic process is described in detail by the authors and practitioners whose schools have profited from its implementation.

Wood, F. H. (1989). Organizing and managing school-based staff development. In S. D. Caldwell (Ed.), *Staff development: A handbook of effective practices* (pp. 26-43). Oxford, OH: National Staff Development Council.

In this chapter, Wood describes the stages of readiness, planning, training, implementation, and maintenance that have become known as the RPTIM model. A section on districtwide staff development for school-based improvement is helpful for central office administrators.

Index

CORWIN
PRESS

The Corwin Press logo—a raven striding across an open book—represents the happy union of courage and learning. We are a professional-level publisher of books and journals for K–12 educators, and we are committed to creating and providing resources that embody these qualities. Corwin's motto is "Success for All Learners."